Brenda—

All the best for
long-term success!

S0-AAZ-057

MARKET EVOLUTION

How to Profit in Today's Changing Financial Markets

Jeffrey Kleintop

WILEY

John Wiley & Sons, Inc.

The opinions and views expressed herein are my own and are not necessarily those of The PNC Financial Services Group, Inc.

Copyright © 2006 by JeffreyKleintop. All rights reserved.

Published by John Wiley & Sons, Inc., Hoboken, New Jersey.
Published simultaneously in Canada.

No part of this publication may be reproduced, stored in a retrieval system, or transmitted in any form or by any means, electronic, mechanical, photocopying, recording, scanning, or otherwise, except as permitted under Section 107 or 108 of the 1976 United States Copyright Act, without either the prior written permission of the Publisher, or authorization through payment of the appropriate per-copy fee to the Copyright Clearance Center, Inc., 222 Rosewood Drive, Danvers, MA 01923, (978) 750-8400, fax (978) 750-4470, or on the web at www.copyright.com. Requests to the Publisher for permission should be addressed to the Permissions Department, John Wiley & Sons, Inc., 111 River Street, Hoboken, NJ 07030, (201) 748-6011, fax (201) 748-6008, or online at http://www.wiley.com/go/permissions.

Limit of Liability/Disclaimer of Warranty: While the publisher and author have used their best efforts in preparing this book, they make no representations or warranties with respect to the accuracy or completeness of the contents of this book and specifically disclaim any implied warranties of merchantability or fitness for a particular purpose. No warranty may be created or extended by sales representatives or written sales materials. The advice and strategies contained herein may not be suitable for your situation. You should consult with a professional where appropriate. Neither the publisher nor author shall be liable for any loss of profit or any other commercial damages, including but not limited to special, incidental, consequential, or other damages.

For general information on our other products and services or for technical support, please contact our Customer Care Department within the United States at (800) 762-2974, outside the United States at (317) 572-3993 or fax (317) 572-4002.

Wiley also publishes its books in a variety of electronic formats. Some content that appears in print may not be available in electronic books. For more information about Wiley products, visit our web site at www.wiley.com.

Library of Congress Cataloging-in-Publication Data

Kleintop, Jeffrey, 1969–
   Market evolution : how to profit in today's changing market / Jeffrey Kleintop.
     p. cm.
   Includes index.
   ISBN-13: 978-0-471-76920-0 (cloth)
   ISBN-10: 0-471-76920-7 (cloth)
   1. Investments. I. Title.
   HG4521.K567 2006
   332.6—dc22

                          2005036106

Printed in the United States of America.

10 9 8 7 6 5 4 3 2 1

for Irene
and
Kendra

Contents

Acknowledgments

I offer my thanks to the many people who helped make *Market Evolution* possible.

I must first thank those without whom I would not have much to say—my team members John Canally, Rebekah McCahan, and Vicky Bagley. John's tireless pursuit of the truth has yielded many of the ideas presented in this book. Rebekah's dedication to getting the job done right has been essential to the development of techniques and insights. And, Vicky's ability to ensure the team operates at top efficiency has been critical to the creation of this book.

The ability to say something is meaningless if you cannot be understood. Thank you, Lorraine Zysk, for laboring to ensure my message is clear. Also, for the past six years Deborah Sullivan has taken pains to make me a better writer. Thank you for your efforts, Deborah; I am sure the readers appreciate it.

I also wish to thank my employer, PNC Financial Services Group, Inc., for affording me the opportunity and resources to share my market insights in this book.

And finally, a special acknowledgment for my family who is used to seeing more of me on television than in person. Thank you for the support and understanding that has allowed me to achieve so much.

About the Author

Jeffrey Kleintop is the Chief Investment Strategist of PNC Advisors, one of the largest wealth managers in the U.S., where he defines the overall investment strategy for thousands of individual and institutional investors with assets totaling $50 billion. Mr. Kleintop also serves as co-portfolio manager of the Advantage Portfolios, the growth, value, and core model stock portfolios used by PNC clients.

Recently cited by the *Wall Street Journal* as one of "Wall Street's Best and Brightest" and known for his keen market insights, he is regularly quoted in many national publications, such as *Business Week* and the *New York Times*, and is a frequent guest on national business television and radio, including CNBC, Bloomberg, and FOX News.

Mr. Kleintop earned his MBA at Penn State, where he has returned as a guest lecturer, and earned a BS in Business Administration with a concentration in Finance from the University of Delaware.

PART I

Adaptation or Extinction

It is not the strongest of the species that survive,
nor the most intelligent, but the one most responsive to change.

—Charles Darwin, British naturalist and author of
The Origin of Species, on the mechanics of evolution
and natural selection 1809–1882.

Investors face a challenging environment today. The drivers of invest-ment performance are undergoing an evolutionary change that is likely to result in financial market performance below the average of recent decades. Such conditions place a premium on adaptation and innova-tion, and make proactive investment decision making more valuable than ever. A new portfolio framework may be necessary to exploit opportunities and achieve performance goals.

An era has ended; a new one has begun. If that is true, then what factors will drive financial markets in the next ten years?

■ A plateau in valuations will evolve from the rising trend of stock and bond valuations in the 1980s and 1990s and declining valua-tions in the early 2000s.
■ More stable inflation and interest rates will evolve from the rela-tively steady decline in both during the past 20 years that drove above-average gains for stocks and bonds.
■ Companies will find new ways to grow earnings and use their assets more efficiently.
■ Dividends are staging a comeback. The decades-long decline in the dividend payout ratio is starting to reverse.

In the environment that confronts investors over the coming years, an adaptive approach to investing is likely to prove to be more valuable

1

than it has been in recent decades. The first section of this book provides insight into where we have been and where we are headed.

Where Have We Been?

The past era—one that spanned 25 years—was great for investors. What made it so great?

- The era began with back-to-back recessions that eventually produced pent up demand by consumers and businesses.
- Interest rates peaked at the start of the 1980s. Falling interest rates and inflation led to rising valuations and above-average rates of return for stocks and bonds.
- Dividends became less important to investors. Earnings became more important to stock valuations, and earnings grew more rapidly than dividends.
- Profit margins rose to new highs as productivity accelerated in the 1990s.
- Business cycles lengthened due to better technology and processes, such as just-in-time inventory management. The business environment became more stable.
- The baby boomers moved into their prime earning years. This demographic shift produced a greater need for saving, and new savings vehicles, like 401(k)s, promoted it.
- The Cold war ended, and the geopolitical environment thawed.

Where Are We Headed?

The next ten years are not likely to match those of the last era.

On the positive side, a shareholder revolution is underway. Companies are more focused on returning value to shareholders than at any time in recent memory. Dividends are growing rapidly, so much so that the composition of the total return for stock is starting to change. For the past 25 years, price appreciation was growing as a percentage of total return at the expense of dividend yield. This relationship is now changing. Two other factors are contributing to the shareholder revolution: share buybacks, which are running at a record-breaking pace, and value-enhancing restructurings. All of these efforts favor stock investors. The last era was marked by a long period in which companies focused on paying down and restructuring debt—a trend that benefited bondholders. In fact, the shareholder revolution may place pressure on bond market performance.

Nevertheless, as the tide turns toward lower returns in the financial markets there is only so much that corporate leaders can do to enhance the performance of the company's shares and debt. One of the reasons that the new era will have a more modest period of stock market performance is that valuations are unlikely to continue to expand. In the past era, their expansion actually drove price appreciation beyond the pace of earnings growth. The bond market will also lose a key driver of return as interest rates maintain a more stable trend.

Another important factor affecting the outlook for investment performance is that many of the factors that affect earnings growth are changing. Over the past two decades, companies benefited from declining interest expenses and declining taxes. With interest rates on the rise and corporate taxes unlikely to fall much further, companies must find alternative ways to drive earnings growth.

Additional factors affecting the financial markets have also experienced changes:

- The strong consumer spending of the past era, even through the 2001 recession, leaves little pent up demand.
- The Cold war has ended, but the war on terror, a different ideological geopolitical conflict, has captured the world's attention.
- The U.S. budget and trade deficits are near record levels. This may place a strain on the world's supply of capital.

It seems difficult to escape the conclusion that we are looking ahead to a new era of lower returns in the financial markets. However, few investors may earn even the lower-than-average returns that lie ahead for the major market indexes. Unfortunately, the research shows that the average investor has a tendency to chase performance. They hold investments for much less than a year and that typically results in performance below the level of the major indexes. Even professionals rarely ever match the returns of the market indexes. Most actively managed mutual funds trail their performance benchmark.

A new breed of investor, armed with insight into the dynamics of the coming era, can avoid the pitfalls of being stuck in the past and invest with confidence. Rather than building a portfolio from the bottom-up, security-by-security, the new breed of investor should embrace evolving markets from the top-down. A forward-thinking, strategic framework with a focus on adaptation is essential to achieve returns close to the long-term averages in this new era of investment performance.

Layout of Section 1

> Stock market performance will be represented most often by the S&P 500®, due to its long history, availability of data, and its good representation of the underlying total stock market. Bonds will most often be measured by the 10-year Treasury Note or intermediate-term Government bonds).

Bond market investment performance is driven primarily by interest rates. There is a very tight relationship between the current yield of a bond and its future performance. Stock market returns are driven by three main factors. The first is valuation—the impact of any change in stock market value relative to earnings (the price-to-earnings ratio). The second is the growth in earnings. And, lastly, the dividends paid to investors.

If we examine the S&P 500 since the end of the Great Depression in March of 1933, we see that the average dividend yield was 5 percent and the average pace of annual earnings growth was 7 percent—together producing the average annual total return of 12 percent. Over the long term, earnings and dividends drive returns, but valuations can magnify or shrink them from year to year—or even decade to decade. During the 1950s, 1980s, and 1990s rising valuations contributed nearly half of the gain in the total return of the S&P 500 Index. During the 1940s, 1960s, and 1970s, falling valuations weakened the contribution of earnings and dividends to total return.

The first three chapters explore the evolution of valuation, earnings growth, and dividends. Chapter 4 provides a historical parallel for our forecasts (the 1960s). And finally, Chapter 5 details the expectations for total returns and volatility for each sub-category of stocks and bonds for the remainder of this business cycle and the next ten years.

CHAPTER 1

Valuation Stabilization

There are three components of stock market total return—valuation, earnings, and dividends. The most important of these has been valuation. In this chapter, I will focus on the following key aspects of valuation:

- The primary driver of valuations, interest rates, suggests relatively stable valuations for stocks and bonds in the coming years in contrast with the large movements of the past 40 years.
- Unlike the prior era, valuations will not be the most potent driver of stock market returns in the new era of investment performance.
- The new era renders tools that investors have used to value stocks in the past, such as the "Fed Model", powerless to provide meaningful investment signals.

Why has valuation been the most important component of total return? A change in the value investors place on earnings and dividends magnifies the changes in these components of return. We can measure this by looking at the price-to-earnings (P/E) ratio, the most common and useful measure of valuation. Over the past 30 years, there have been 21 periods when the stock market, measured by the S&P 500, has risen or fallen by more than 10 percent. On average, the expansion or contraction in the price-to-earnings ratio has accounted for over 60 percent of the market's performance during these periods.

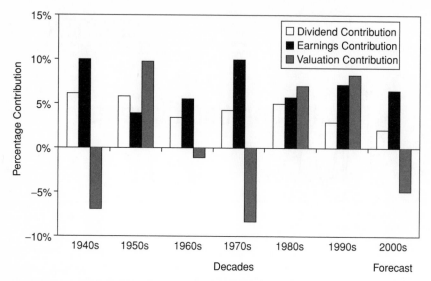

FIGURE 1.1   S&P 500 total return components by decade.
Percentage contribution to total return for decade.

Although market cycles do not fall neatly into decades, sometimes it can be useful to look at market history by decade (see Figure 1.1). Stocks rose every decade from the 1940s through the 1990s. While earnings and dividends have demonstrated a stable trend across the decades, valuations have varied widely. Valuations acted as a drag on returns in 1940s, 1960s, and 1970s, and boosted returns in the 1950s,1980s and 1990s. The net impact of changes in valuation over the very long term has been close to zero, but for extended periods the changes can be quite meaningful. In fact, during the 1980s and 1990s we witnessed a valuation expansion that made up nearly half of the total return on the S&P 500 index.

While earnings are up 35 percent since the start of 2000, stocks are still in negative territory. It is likely that earnings and dividends will make up all of the total return of the S&P 500 in this decade much as they did in the 1960s.

Drivers of Valuation

If valuation (see Figure 1.2) has acted as the dominant force driving stock market performance, then what drives valuation? Several factors

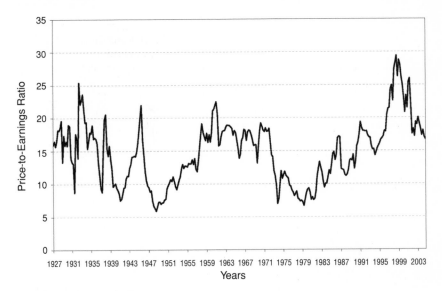

FIGURE 1.2   Stock market valuation.
S&P 500 price-to-earnings ratio on last four quarters operating earnings.

may make investors willing to afford the stock market a higher valuation. In other words, under some conditions investors may be willing to
pay a little more for each dollar of current earnings. These factors include
changes in:

Expected earnings growth—In general, valuations expand when
    earnings growth has slowed and is expected to reaccelerate, and
    valuations fall as earnings growth is rising but expected to fade.
Investor risk tolerance—Valuations often decline when investors
    fear the impact of certain types of current events, such as mili-
    tary conflicts, natural disasters, and political changes. When
    faced with a higher degree of uncertainty, investors are gener-
    ally less willing to take on risk. Alternatively, valuations often
    rise when investors perceive positive changes, such as deesca-
    lating geopolitical conflict or improving corporate governance.
The outlook for interest rates and inflation—The current value of
    future earnings falls as inflation and interest rates rise. Higher
    inflation and interest rates erode the value of future profits.
    Lower rates preserve more of the future value of profits. For
    example, let's compare what $10 in profits earned ten years

from now is worth today, using different interest rates to discount the future earnings. At a 4 percent interest rate—the average yield on the ten-year Treasury Note in 2005—$10 in future
profits is worth $68 today. At a 16 percent interest rate—the
peak in the ten-year Treasury Note yield in the early 1980s—the
$10 profit is worth only $23 today. All else being equal, rising
interest rates result in lower valuations and falling rates result in
higher valuations.

The last of these factors, interest rates, has been the most potent
driver of valuations over time. This has been true in part because
changes in interest rates tend to capture to some of the changes in
investors' risk tolerance and growth expectations.

Interest-ing Effect

Today, one of the most significant differences from the prior era of
investing is the outlook for interest rates, which have been a major factor affecting the performance of many types of investments. Measured
by the yield on the ten-year Treasury Note, interest rates rose in the late
1960s and throughout the 1970s, peaked in the early 1980s, and then
steadily fell over the past 25 years. The period of rising interest rates
produced very different rates of return for investors than the period of
falling interest rates. See Figure 1.3.

The relatively modest rise in rates from 1960 to around 1968 accompanied a trend-like gain of 11 percent for the stock market. However,
from 1968 until September of 1981, when interest rates were rising
sharply, the major stock market indexes were volatile but remained
essentially unchanged, leaving the total return on stocks to track the
dividend yield of around 5 percent. Bonds provided a total return of
about 5 percent per year. Then, as interest rates fell from their peak,
financial market returns rebounded. Bonds posted above-average performance of 9.3 percent on an annualized basis and stocks posted
above-average returns of 13.3 percent.

In the past, the outlook for inflation has been the primary driver of
changes in interest rates. In general, when expectations for inflation
are on the rise, investments tend to perform poorly. This is because
inflation erodes value. At a 5 percent expected rate of inflation, the
value of a $10 bond over ten years is only $61 in today's terms. A higher

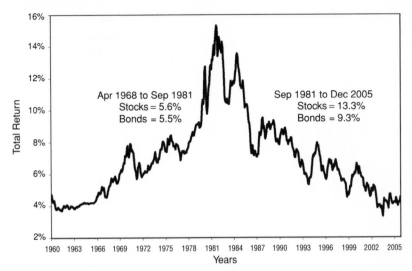

FIGURE 1.3 The rise and fall of interest rates.
Yield on 10-year treasury note with total return on S&P 500 and Ibbotson U.S.
Intermediate-Term Bond Index.

expected rate of inflation would result in a lower current value for the bond, while a lower expected rate would preserve more value over time. Because financial markets are forward-looking, future expectations about inflation drive security prices even more than the current pace of inflation.

The relationship between expected inflation and interest rates has been very tight. After spending much of the 1950s and 1960s in a low, stable range, inflation began to rise in the late 1960s and really soared in the 1970s, sending interest rates much higher. While inflation peaked in early 1980 at a year-over-year rise of 15.8 percent, rising inflation expectations pushed interest rates higher until September of 1981, when the yield on the ten-year Treasury Note reached 15.8 percent. Inflation fell quickly in the early 1980s and has averaged 3.1 percent since 1982 (see Figure 1.4). However, after witnessing the destructive effects of inflation, investors were hesitant to lower their expectations for future inflation. Consequently, the inflation expectations reflected in bond yields receded much more slowly than the actual pace of inflation. At the end of 1982, inflation was running at a pace of 3.8 percent, yet the yield on the ten-year Treasury Bond was 10.4 percent. The vast majority of the difference, or spread, between the two was based on fears of a resurgence in inflation.

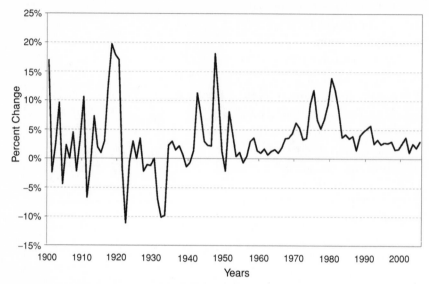

FIGURE 1.4 Inflation has become tamer.
Year-over-year change in Consumer Price Index.

In the early part of the twentieth century, inflation was volatile. Its movement was, in part, tied to war—big jumps in inflation during periods of conflict were followed by sharp declines. After World War II, inflation remained low and stable through the 1960s. Around the start of the 1970s, inflation began to creep higher steadily. After 1971, gold no longer backed the value of the U.S. dollar. As a result, the Federal Reserve Board's policymakers had greater flexibility to increase the money supply. To counter the negative effects of the 1973 Arab Oil Embargo that lead to a quadrupling of oil prices by 1974 and the 1979 Iranian Revolution that led to another tripling of oil prices, the Fed increased the money supply. In fact, the supply of money grew much faster than the output of goods and services, putting upward pressure on the prices of most goods and services.

Recognizing their error, the Fed initiated policies in late 1979 to lower inflation by controlling the growth rate of the money supply. The policies worked. Inflation, which had hit a year-over-year high of 14.8 percent in March 1980, fell to 8.9 percent by the end of 1981, and tumbled to below 4 percent by the end of 1982. In the 1990s and 2000s, productivity-oriented process improvements in corporate America led to greater operating efficiencies, which helped to keep inflation in a range of 1 percent to 4 percent. The lessons on inflation learned by policy-makers during the 1970s were very painful. History is unlikely to repeat itself anytime soon.

Throughout the 1980s, 1990s and into the early 2000s, the decline in inflation led to slowly declining interest rates and a lengthy period of above-average investment performance. The valuation of the stock market, measured by the price-to-earnings ratio of the S&P 500 Index, rose from below ten to well over 20. Why did this happen?

In the early 1980s, stocks were competing with double-digit yields on bonds and even on money market funds. Investors required higher returns to entice them to buy stocks; this kept valuations relatively low. Today, bond yields are around 4 percent. With competitive investments offering lower returns, stock investors require lower rates of return, which supports higher valuations.

During the 1980s and 1990s, stocks posted above-average annualized returns. From the end of 1982 through 1999, stocks returned 18 percent—well ahead of their 12 percent long-term average. The period's annualized 18 percent return was driven mostly by a doubling of valuations (measured by P/E—price-to-earnings ratio). Earnings growth contributed 7 percent, and dividends added 4 percent.

Looking ahead, interest rates are unlikely to go much lower, but a resurgence to the levels of the 1970s is also unlikely. Instead, a relatively low, stable range for interest rates—much like that experienced during the 1950s and early 1960s—is likely in the years ahead.

The End of the Long Decline in Interest Rates

While some degree of variation in interest rates within a business cycle still will take place, the long-term decline across the business cycles has ended now that rates are in line with historic lows. There are several reasons why the yield on the 10-year Treasury note of just above 3 percent seen in mid-2003 may mark the end of the decline:

The rate of productivity growth—An increase in productivity, output per hour, is a downward force on inflation. The current rate of productivity growth is around the long-term average of 2.5 percent. Productivity growth surged to a 5 percent annual pace in late 2003, a healthy rebound from the low 1 percent average rate of the mid-1970s through the mid-1990s. Productivity is unlikely to contribute to further declines in inflation and, thus, interest rates.

The supply of government bonds—The large federal budget deficit and the re-issuance of the 30-year Treasury Bond are likely to result in a steady supply of government bonds, a reversal from the dwindling supply of longer-maturity bonds of recent years. When supply is high, prices are low and, for bonds, lower prices lead to higher yields.

Record trade imbalance—The imbalance in the U.S. current account reflects a large trade deficit with the rest of the world. In 2004, the United States borrowed a record $700 billion from the rest of the world. In 2004 and 2005, the supply of capital available to the United States has been abundant, which has kept interest rates low. However, signs are beginning to appear that the global flow of capital may be in the early stages of reversing. The supply of capital to the U.S. may decrease. When supply goes down, prices go up. Thus, in the United States the price of capital—interest rates—may rise.

The final point deserves some additional exploration. Over the long-term, international capital should naturally flow from developed nations to developing countries. Capital flowing out of slower-growing developed nations to seek better investment opportunities may generate higher returns, which developed countries can use to support their higher share of retirees per worker. Capital flowing into developing nations promotes economic growth in those countries and eventually produces higher living standards for their younger work forces.

However, during the past ten years developing countries that were once net borrowers of international capital, such as Korea, Thailand, Brazil, Argentina, and some countries in parts of Africa, Eastern Europe, and the Middle East, became lenders. During this time, mature slower-growing countries like the United States became net borrowers. See Figure 1.5

This unlikely transposition took place after a series of crises in the developing world cut off capital flows to developing markets. It began in 1994 with Mexico's peso crisis, worsened during Asia's financial crisis in 1997 and Russia's bond default in 1998, and ended in 2002 with Argentina's record-breaking debt default. With little access to capital, develop-

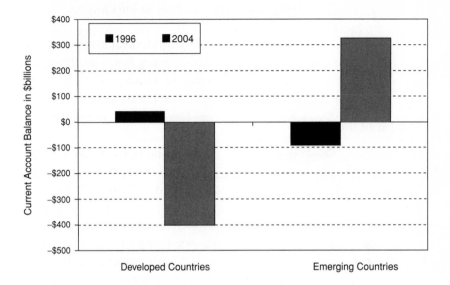

FIGURE 1.5 Role reversal.
Global current account balances by classification.

ing economies grew through exports and were able to develop large capital reserves to lend to the rest of the world.

Nevertheless, it is likely that capital flows will begin to return to normal patterns. Many developing countries are seeking to invest in capital-intensive industries, in response to the strong global demand for the commodities that they produce. While developing nations have been net lenders in the past decade, their demand for international capital seems poised to rise because they now are able to access capital on relatively good terms.

Following a U.S. appeals court ruling in May 2005, the Argentine government completed the biggest debt restructuring in history by exchanging its defaulted bonds for new securities. This is a key step in restoring investor confidence and paves the way for Argentina to begin tapping into international capital markets. In early 2005, Russia's long-term foreign debt rating was raised to BBB– by Standard and Poor's, the global debt-rating agency. For the first time in the country's history and in marked improvement from the 1998 default, Russian government debt no longer bears the "junk bond" stigma.

The normalization of lending and borrowing among developed and developing countries may take years. In the interim, as developed and developing economies compete for capital, the global demand for capital will increase. As demand rises, so do prices for capital; and that means an end to the downward pressure on interest rates.

No Repeat of the 1970s

With interest rates near 40-year lows, we are unlikely to experience further substantial declines. However, interest rates are also not likely to rise sharply like they did in the 1970s because inflation is unlikely to soar to the levels seen in the 1970s or early 1980s. A few reasons include:

Ongoing productivity gains—Productivity is likely to grow at its long-term 2.5 percent pace given ongoing technology and process improvements, combined with an aging and more experienced workforce. As mentioned before, an increase in productivity growth is a downward force on inflation. A steady rate of growth near the long-term average would likely be inflation-neutral and interest-rate neutral.

Containment of labor costs from outsourcing—Ample and growing global supply of labor is likely to keep a lid on wages, the largest component of corporate costs, putting less upward pressure on prices.

A capacity and willingness to lend by individuals and institutions— Capital remains abundant, which keeps borrowing costs, or interest rates, low.

A vigilant Federal Reserve with a focus on price stability—The Federal Reserve has proven itself as an effective inflation fighter, maintaining a low and steady rate of inflation for over ten years.

Limited inflationary effect from high energy prices—Energy prices have risen, threatening to fuel inflation. However, the painful lessons learned in the 1970s when the Fed exacerbated the inflationary impact of high energy prices are unlikely to be repeated. Also, the risk to inflation posed by high energy prices is not what it used to be, since the U.S. economy is much less oil intensive than it was decades ago, when price spikes spread quickly throughout the economy. The U.S. needed nearly one and a half barrels of oil to generate $1,000 of real GDP in the 1950s, 1960s, and 1970s. Today, the larger and more information-oriented U.S. economy consumes only a little more than a half of a barrel to produce $1,000 of real GDP, or a little more than a third as much as it used to (see Figure 1.6). Energy costs for most corporations are now fairly small, at just 1–2 percent, and energy makes up about 5–6 percent of consumers' budgets. Energy prices have been rising for several years, yet consumer prices excluding energy have remained on a steady 2 percent trend.

Interest rates have fallen from 16 percent in 1982 to 4 percent in 2005. With interest rates in line with historic lows, it is unlikely that rates will continue to steadily fall.

Tying It Together

Valuation has acted as the dominant force driving stock market performance and interest rates have been the most potent driver of valuations over time. Interest rates are near 40-year lows and unlikely to

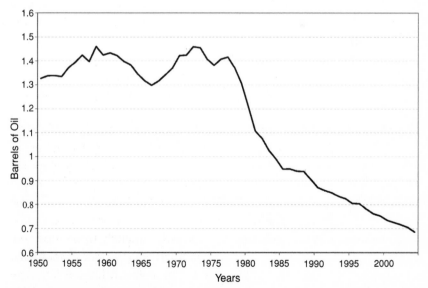

FIGURE 1.6   Oil intensity of GDP.
Number of barrels of oil to produce $1,000 of real Gross Domestic Product.

experience further substantial declines. So, what conclusions should we reach about valuations in this new era of investing?

First, valuations will not be the most potent driver of stock market returns, as they were in the 1980s and 1990s when falling interest rates drove P/E ratios higher. During the next ten years, the stock market is likely to exhibit a price-to-earnings ratio range of 14 to 22, as it did during the 1960s. In the future, valuations will take a back seat. Earnings growth and, to a lesser extent, dividends, will drive stock market returns in the new era of investing.

Bond Valuations

Bond valuations are directly tied to interest rates—so closely, in fact, that interest rates are a great predictor of future investment performance for the bond market. The yield on the intermediate-term government bond index has accurately forecast the performance of that index over the subsequent ten years. The relationship is very tight. Measured statistically, the correlation is a very high 0.91 since 1926. See Figure 1.7.

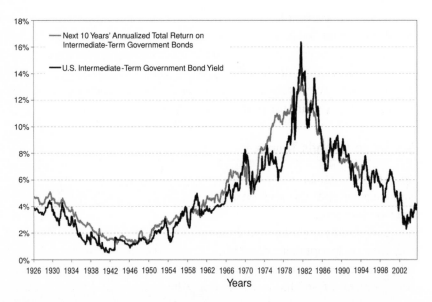

FIGURE 1.7   Yields predict bond returns.
Intermediate-term government bond yield and next 10 years annualized total return on intermediate-term government bonds.

TABLE 1.1   Median Total Returns at Different Interest Rates
Total Return on S&P 500 and US Intermediate Term Bonds
from 1954 to 2005

Yield on 10-Year Treasury Note	Next Twelve Months Median Total Return	
	Stocks	Bonds
2–3%	35.5%	0.0%
3–4%	17.1%	2.8%
4–5%	8.5%	3.8%
5–6%	9.0%	4.4%
6–7%	8.3%	6.2%
7–8%	11.3%	8.9%
8–9%	16.5%	9.1%
9–10%	19.0%	10.0%
10–11%	25.4%	6.4%
11–12%	10.8%	13.0%
>12%	18.9%	12.2%

Given the current level of interest rates, the total return on the bond market over the next ten years is likely to be in the mid-single digits. The period of above-average bond returns driven by the long decline in interest rates may finally be at an end. The falling interest rates of the last 25 years have resulted in returns double those likely to be achieved in the next ten years for both bonds and stocks. See Table 1.1.

Stocks and Bonds Together

Not only are stock and bond valuations changing due to interest rates and inflation, but the relationship between the stock and bond markets is also changing.

Correlation measures the degree to which asset returns move together or in opposite directions. Over time, the correlation between two asset classes can change. For instance, the relationship between the total returns of stocks and the total return of bonds has varied over the past 75 years. During much of the 1980s and 1990s, stock and bond prices generally moved together, as reflected in the +0.5 correlation between them over the period. In recent years, just as in the 1950s, the correlation of stock and bond returns reversed, reaching −0.5. See Figure 1.8.

I expect the correlation between stocks and bonds to rise modestly, but to remain below the levels seen in the 1980s and 1990s. Because bond prices fall as interest rates rise, lower correlation between stock prices and bond prices is the same as a higher correlation between stock prices and bond yields. In an era of a low, stable pace of inflation relative to historical levels, the volatility of interest rates may be driven more by expectations for the real rate of economic growth than by inflation expectations.

In general, rising inflation tends to be a negative for both stocks and bonds. In contrast, rising real growth is a plus for stocks but a negative for bonds, because it drives bond yields higher and prices fall. A similar period of negative correlation between stock and bond prices resulting from low and stable inflation occurred in the 1950s and 1960s.

The new era renders tools that investors have used to value stocks in the past, such as the "Fed Model", powerless to provide meaningful investment signals. Though the methodology of the "Fed Model" had been in use for a long time, it got its name from a July 1997 report to

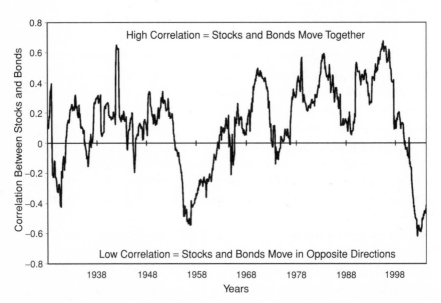

FIGURE 1.8   Dynamic relationship.
Correlation between stocks and bonds.

Congress by the Federal Reserve. The report highlighted the close relationship between the yield of the ten-year Treasury Note and the earnings yield of the S&P 500 (the earnings yield is simply the earnings-to-price ratio, or the inverse of the price-to-earnings ratio), with the implication that this was a model the Federal Reserve is using to value the stock market. The model implies that stocks and bonds compete with each other and that the yield on bonds and the yield on stocks (measured by earnings rather than dividends) may remain equal. This suggests a negative relationship between stock price and bond yields (or a positive relationship between stock prices and bond prices, since the yield on a bond moves in the opposite direction of the price)— when bond yields rise, stocks must drop in price in order to raise the earnings yield to match the bond yield. However, since bond yields and stock prices are now more likely to move in the same direction this tool is rendered ineffective.

A benefit of the changing correlation between stocks and bonds is that as price volatility rises in the years ahead from cycle lows, a lower-than-average correlation between bonds and stocks should produce more benefits from diversification, which should serve to moderate overall portfolio volatility.

A Valuable Lesson

The period of above-average returns for the financial markets driven by the long decline in interest rates may finally be at an end. Bonds are likely to offer only mid-single-digit returns. This is due to the fact that interest rates are unlikely to go much lower with the yield on the ten-year Treasury Note having come down from 16 percent in the early 1980s to stand now near 40-year lows of around 4 percent. Instead interest rates may drift higher over the remainder of the decade, acting as a drag on returns. With bonds likely to offer performance in line with yields, it is likely that bonds will return 4 to 6 percent in the next ten years—just half of the gains experienced in the prior era.

With valuations stable in the years ahead, stocks are likely to track earnings growth of 7 percent, roughly half the pace of performance offered investors over the past 25 years. We will explore the changing nature of earnings growth, the key driver of stock market performance, in the next chapter.

CHAPTER 2

Earnings Growth

Over long periods, stock price performance correlates highly with earnings expectations—more so than with other variables, like interest rates. As highlighted in the prior chapter, changes in valuation do have a magnifying effect on stock market price performance, but the underlying driver of that performance remains the growth in profits. This chapter examines the key factors driving earnings growth.

■ The outlook for the long-term earnings growth rate of 7 percent, well below the long-term average of 12 percent.
■ The saw-tooth cyclical pattern of earnings growth.
■ An evolutionary shift in the key driver of earnings growth to Asset Turnover.

Assessing the earnings outlook for any one company depends on many factors, including the challenges of predicting changes in market share within the industry, changes in specific input costs or the prices of unique products, and the demand for a specific good or service by consumers. However, this assessment has become more challenging as technology has led to an increase in the pace of innovation—competitive advantages have become more fleeting. As a result, the companies among the top earnings growers in an industry are changing more rapidly.

Fortunately, when looking at the big picture many earnings factors cancel each other out. For every firm that gains market share in an industry, another loses market share. One company's costs are often another company's profits. Aggregate consumer spending is fairly stable. It is generally easier to place more confidently a narrower band of earnings expectations on the stock market as a whole, or at least the large U.S. companies that make up the S&P 500 Index and most of the value of the U.S. stock market, than on any one company.

Long Term Earnings Growth of Seven Percent

The long-term trend of earnings growth for the companies in the S&P 500 has been 7 percent. Each earnings cycle since 1937 has closely averaged around 7 percent earnings growth. The only exception was the cycle ending in September of 1959—an unusually short cycle lasting less than half as long as the average cycle that contained an economic recession during the middle quarters. However, given the cyclical nature of earnings, they have rarely grown precisely 7 percent in any one year. Over time, earnings have not strayed far from the trend for long. See Figure 2.1. See the appendix on quality of earnings for why S&P 500 operating earnings are a reliable measure of profits and basis for valuation.

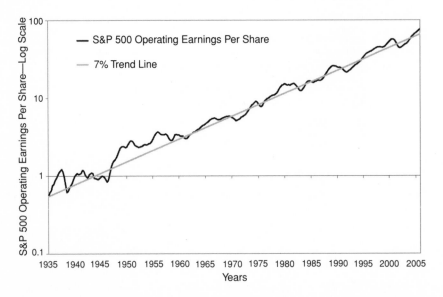

FIGURE 2.1   S&P 500 earnings per share growth has been 7% over the long-term. S&P 500 earnings per share (sum of last four quarters) and 7% trend line—logarithmic scale.

The 7 percent growth trend can also be measured between earnings cycle peaks. For example, from the 1981 earnings peak to the 1989 earnings peak, operating earnings-per-share rose at a 7 percent annualized rate. Likewise, earnings-per-share grew at a 7 percent rate from the 1989 peak to the 2000 peak. It is hard to argue with that track record. I believe that S&P 500 operating earnings will average 7 percent growth for this earnings cycle (which will likely last through the end of this decade) and most likely the next cycle, as well.

Interestingly, the average pace of 7 percent earnings growth has been consistent regardless of the rate of inflation. For instance, during the earnings cycle that ended in 1981, inflation averaged a very high 9 percent. During the earnings cycles that ended in 1989 and 2000, inflation averaged around 3 percent. Yet in each cycle, earnings growth was around 7 percent. See Figure 2.2.

As noted in Chapter 1, inflation is likely to remain at 2 to 3 percent, which is in line with the pace of the past couple of cycles. Although this pace of inflation is below the long-term average of 4.5 percent, it does not necessarily follow that earnings will grow at a slower pace than the long-term average. Why? In general, companies in the S&P 500

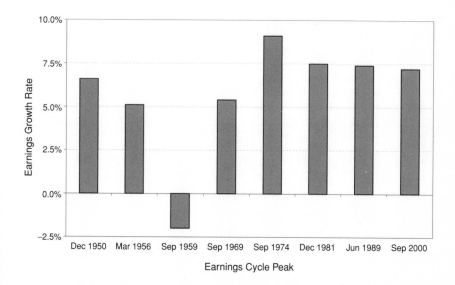

FIGURE 2.2 Annualized earnings growth by cycle.
Percent growth in operating earnings per share from peak of prior cycle 1937-2000.

have adapted successfully to different inflation environments, enabling them collectively to maintain a consistent 7 percent pace of earnings growth across cycles with different levels of inflation. See Table 2.1.

Saw-Tooth Pattern

Even with a forecast that S&P 500 operating earnings will average 7 percent growth in this earnings cycle and most likely the next, the pattern of earnings growth in the coming years is likely to be anything but constant. Earnings growth over the remainder of this cycle should adhere to its typical cyclical pattern, which is irregular or saw-toothed.

A typical earnings cycle has three stages that result in a double peak (the sawteeth). Historically, each earnings cycle has generally consisted of:

- A rebound from recession to more than 20 percent growth.
- A mid-cycle pause in growth.
- A resumption of growth to 20 percent or higher again as the cycle draws to a close.

The repeating pattern of earnings growth is evident in Figure 2.3 and it is the result of the different stages of the business cycle. Also, the pattern is related to challenges to growth that are often present in the mid-to-later stages of the business cycle. The familiar saw-tooth pat-

TABLE 2.1   Earnings Growth Unaffected by Inflation
Earnings Growth and Inflation by Earnings Cycle from 1937 to 2000

Earnings Cycle Peak	Prior Four Quarters Earnings in $	Annualized Earnings Growth from Prior Cycle Peak in %	Annualized Pace of Inflation from Prior Cycle Peak in %
Sep 1937	1.22		
Dec 1950	2.84	6.6	4.2
Mar 1956	3.69	5.1	1.4
Sep 1959	3.43	−2.0	2.5
Sep 1969	5.89	5.4	2.4
Sep 1974	9.11	9.1	6.1
Dec 1981	15.36	7.5	8.9
Jun 1989	26.18	7.4	3.8
Sep 2000	57.33	7.2	3.0

tern of earnings growth seems to be repeating during the current cycle, although the width (time span) of the teeth of earnings growth may expand or contract.

Earnings growth has slowed in 2005 and is likely to continue to slow in 2006 and 2007. However, the stock market has generally climbed during the mid-cycle pause in earnings growth during past earnings cycles. In fact, during the mid-cycle earnings growth slowdowns that occurred in mid-1980 and mid-1990, the S&P 500 posted an annualized total return of 29 percent! Thus, the S&P 500 may be on a path to reach a new high in mid-2008.

It is important to understand the history and pattern of earnings growth when formulating an earnings outlook. However, even given the very consistent track-record earnings growth, to assume that history will repeat itself ignores the evolution in the drivers of earnings growth. There are several significant differences in the underlying drivers of growth. For instance, many corporate leaders are facing the negative effects of the end of a long decline in interest and tax expenses, rising tort liability, and increased regulations governing corporate risk-taking. However, they also stand to benefit from growth in productivity and

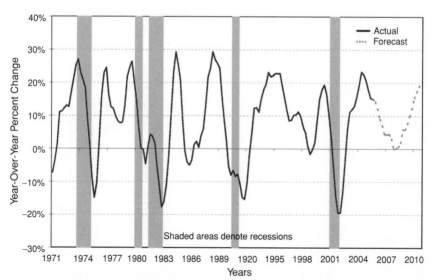

FIGURE 2.3 Saw-tooth earnings pattern.
S&P 500 operating earnings year-over-year percent change of four quarter sum.

contained labor costs and, most important, a turnaround in the 30-year trend for the ratio of sales-to-assets, known as "asset turnover."

Interest Expenses

The decline in interest rates over the past 25 years has had a significant impact on corporate earnings. Interest expense for U.S. corporations fell from 50 percent of pre-tax income in the early 1980s to the teens today. This decline in interest expense acted as a boost to earnings growth. See Figure 2.4.

It is possible that we have seen the low point of interest rates for the rest of this decade (and perhaps several to follow). At around 4 percent, yields remain close to 40-year lows after reaching nearly 16 percent in the early 1980s. With interest rates unlikely to fall, earnings will not experience the same boost from declining interest expense enjoyed over the past 25 years.

Even if interest rates declined, it is unlikely that corporate interest expense would fall by much, given recent changes in corporate liabil-

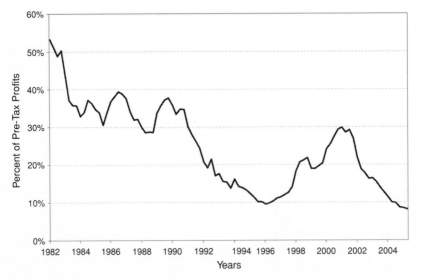

Figure 2.4   Declining interest expense as a percent of pre-tax profits has boosted profits.
U.S. companies' net interest as a percentage of pre-tax profits.

ity structure. For the past 40 years, the ratio of long-term debt to short-term corporate debt has averaged 1.5, ranging from one to two. In other words, companies typically had one and a half times as much long-term debt as short-term debt. Recently, the ratio has soared to 4.0 as corporations have taken advantage of low long-term rates (see Figure 2.5). In many cases, companies refinanced their debt to ensure that they would not have to roll over maturing debt in the next few years. Given that interest rates are more likely to rise than fall, companies that did refinance have stabilized, to some extent, their interest expenses. They may be in good position to avoid rising interest payments that could otherwise become a drag on their earnings. Nevertheless, it appears that the long period in which declining interest expense actually boosted earnings growth has finally ended.

Tax Expenses

While death remains a certainty for us all, taxes have proven to be somewhat more flexible, especially for corporations. Over the past 25 years, taxes as a percentage of corporate pre-tax income have fallen

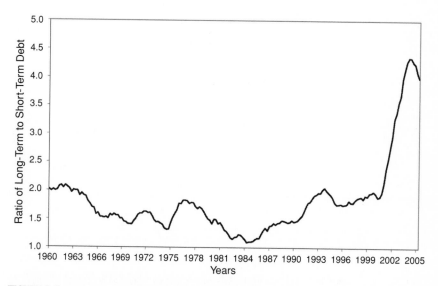

FIGURE 2.5   Long-term debt replacing short-term debt.
Long-term to short-term total debt of non-financial corporations.

from 45 percent to 25 percent, lowering expenses and boosting profit margin growth. The secular downward trend in tax expense as a percentage of pre-tax income is the result of changes in both U.S. fiscal policy and corporate structure. This benefit has accelerated in recent years, given:

- Increased depreciation allowances.
- Liberalization of the use of tax losses.
- Offshore domiciling of businesses, exposing them to lower tax rates outside the United States (i.e., Bermuda).

However, this downward trend is not likely to continue because previous tax cuts have been substantial and because:

- An important bonus feature of depreciation—which permitted corporations to borrow forward tax benefits from future years—expired at the end of 2004.
- Foreign subsidiary tax benefits for U.S. companies have been repealed.
- The tax deductions associated with exercising options may fade, not because of changes in tax code, but because of changes in accounting rules that require that granted options be expensed may lead companies to provide fewer options grants to employees.

It is unlikely the effective corporate tax rate will fall significantly further because that would require a radical change or changes in the U.S. tax structure. Therefore, the earnings boost that corporations enjoy from falling tax expenses, much like from falling interest expenses, is likely to fade.

More Conservative Management

For the typical U.S. company, the combination of all types of commodities—from steel to gasoline to chemicals to corn—only amount to around 5 percent of business expenses. While energy prices often garner much attention, energy commodities make up only around half of that total, roughly in line with legal expenses. This makes for an interesting comparison which suggests that legal costs may pose a significant risk to corporate earnings growth in the new era.

Energy costs as a percent of total expenses have been declining over the long-term. On the other hand, legal costs have risen. In fact, according to the actuarial and consulting firm, Tillinghast-Towers Perrin, U.S. tort costs (legal damages for which a civil suit can be brought) have grown at an annualized pace of 10 percent over the past 50 years and are now equivalent to nearly 2.5 percent of GDP. In other words, a significant cost for corporations is rising at an incredible pace. See Figure 2.6.

The steady rise in tort costs has been the result of several factors, including the increasing frequency of class-action lawsuits and large claim awards, record jury awards in medical malpractice and personal injury cases, and an increase in the number and size of shareholder lawsuits.

Besides the direct outlays for settlements and jury awards, tort costs impact businesses through employee healthcare costs, which have been rising much faster than wages for some time. One reason for rising healthcare costs is the increase in medical malpractice costs, which have risen 12 percent per year on average since 1975, outpacing the 9

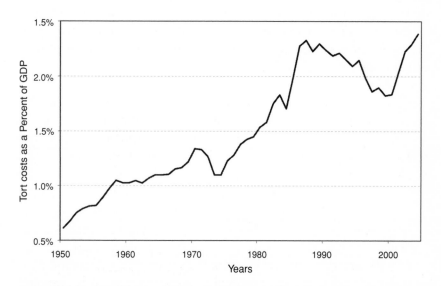

FIGURE 2.6 Tort costs are equivalent to nearly 2.5% of U.S. economic output. Tort costs as a percent of GDP.

Source: Towers Perrin.

percent average annual rise in overall tort costs excluding medical mal-practice. Rising tort costs also indirectly affect corporate earnings through increased legal reserves and soaring premiums for corporate directors' insurance.

Rising legal costs are a risk to corporate earnings growth and may increasingly act as a drag, particularly in some industries. At the extreme, the risk of soaring legal liability could leave many industries, like pharmaceuticals and restaurants, following the path of asbestos and tobacco producers. It is possible that increased legal costs could result in less risk-taking across all of corporate America. Given that the rate at which a company generates profits is tied to its successful undertaking of risk, less risk-taking would ultimately lower long-term earnings growth rates. Within corporations, the centers of influence may shift among members of corporate executive teams. The Chief Risk Officer may have more impact on financial results than the Chief Financial Officer. The key qualification to becoming a Chief Executive Officer may soon be a law degree and not an MBA (just ask former attorney Chuck Prince, now CEO of Citigroup).

Compounding the impact of rising legal liability is a post-account-ing- scandal environment in which newly energized shareholders, auditors, and boards are more closely examining every executive decision, potentially creating a more conservative bias to business decision making than what took place during the 1990s. The evolving business climate could lead to:

- Less aggressive capacity spending—Burned by overcapacity in the downturn, business leaders may shy away from growth-at-any-cost strategies.
- More dividends—Returning cash to shareholders in the form of dividends and buybacks, rather than reinvesting in the business, corporations may take a more disciplined approach to using cash flow.
- Less debt—The excesses in the form of higher leverage were dramatic during the prior business cycle. The growth in corporate debt as a percentage of net worth surged as corporations issued debt to buy back stock and finance expensive acquisitions. The combination of low inflation and a high degree of leverage is a bad one for many stocks, and may mean more bankruptcies and hindered growth for highly indebted companies.

■ More transparency—Accounting practices will offer greater clarity into underlying business fundamentals because investors are likely to apply discounts to those with complicated or questionable accounting. S&P 500 operating earnings will track cash flow more closely than in the past.

Business decision makers may adapt their strategies to rising legal liabilities by taking a more conservative approach to the generation of earnings. However, the negative effects are likely to be mitigated by more efficient and focused profit growth rather than the wasteful aggressive pursuit of revenues that characterized the slide in profit margins in the late 1990s.

Re-Regulation

A defining feature of the prior era was that of deregulation. Across many industries, including airlines, telecommunications, banking, and utilities, the past two decades featured a progressive withdrawal of government from direct involvement in the economy. Productivity, cost restraint, low inflation, and long business upsurges resulted as companies focused on competitive creation of wealth for shareholders. Unfortunately, too much of a good thing led to unsatisfactory results because each of these industries eventually ran into trouble.

■ The Telecommunications Act of 1996 required local monopolies to open their markets to competitors in exchange for approval to sell long-distance service. The deregulation efforts ushered in hundreds of competitors, choking the industry with irrational competition and leaving carriers with ill-equipped business models.
■ The deregulation of public utilities has met with mixed success. In California in the 1990s, efforts to deregulate utilities in order to spur competition and lower costs instead resulted in electric utilities facing a financial crisis; consumers were met with electricity shortages and skyrocketing prices. The Public Utility Holding Company Act was passed during the Great Depression in response to the failure of a number of utility holding companies after they defrauded investors. This act will likely be reformed to effectively address mar-

ket power abuses, prevent cross-subsidization, and preserve fair competition. A slower pace of deregulation can be expected.

■ The airlines were deregulated 30 years ago. Since then, airfares have fallen dramatically and competition on major routes has risen. But the state of the airline industry is such that it requires support.

■ Until about 30 years ago, balance was maintained between a financial company's investment bank and its brokerage business because commissions for stock trading were fixed. Trading fees kept the brokerage business disproportionately profitable and, to a large degree, preserved the autonomy of analysts who worked for brokerage clients. When a federal law made commissions float in 1975, commissions fell and research became beholden to investment banking. New regulation may be introduced to insulate research from investment banking.

More effective regulation—achieved by putting teeth in the good existing regulations and reforming others—is likely to replace the rampant deregulation that marked the prior era. While re-regulation in the short-term may slow earnings growth, the elimination of conflicts of interest and those factors that facilitate unethical behavior will serve to build confidence and avert the value destruction that can result from ineffective regulation.

Also, the relatively new Office of Homeland Security may have as profound an impact and influence on the structure of our economy in the decade ahead as the Environmental Protection Agency had a few decades back with federal intervention in the airline industry, the insurance industry, and banking.

Productivity and Labor Costs

A key driver that will help offset these negative effects of rising interest and tax expenses, tort costs, and regulation is the mid-1990s return to 2 percent productivity growth after a 20-year absence. Productivity improvement can be defined as more output per unit of input. For the past 100 years, output per worker (industrial production divided by non-farm workers) has averaged 2.5 percent (see Figure 2.7). Only the Great Depression and the inflation bubble of the 70s and 80s have interrupted this trend. This renewed trend in productivity growth, along with

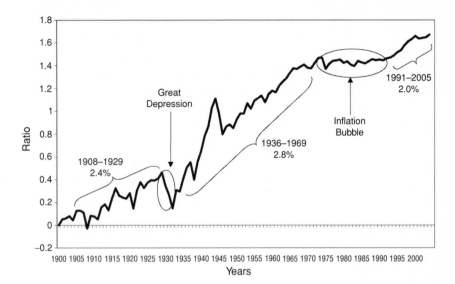

FIGURE 2.7   Long-term productivity trend.
Ratio of industrial production to non-farm payrolls.

an abundant global labor supply, is likely to keep the growth in cost of labor per unit of output low. This is significant since labor is the principal component of total business expenses.

The 2.5 percent trend growth rate in productivity should remain intact despite a growing proportion of spending on defense. While defense spending as a percentage of GDP has fallen over the past 40 years, recently it has started to rise. Rather than act as a drag on resources slowing productivity growth, in fact, defense spending has a positive effect on productivity in the long-term because many technologies developed by the military eventually make their way into civilian applications.

Productivity helps boost profit margins. In many cases, as productivity increases, less labor input is required to produce more output. This is significant because labor makes up 70 percent of business expenses for U.S. companies.

Where Will Earnings Come From?

Profit margins have reached new highs early in this business cycle. Now that we are at the start of a new era of lower returns for all major asset classes, stock market price performance will likely track earnings growth of around 7 percent. If that is true, what will drive earnings growth in the future? Successful U.S. companies will be those that are leaner, contain intangible asset growth, and use new technologies and processes to improve the efficiency of existing assets.

To arrive at this conclusion, the first step is to separate earnings growth into its four key relationships:

■ Profit margin—The ratio of net income to sales, which measures how much profit a company makes for each good or service sold.
■ Retention ratio—The percentage of a company's earnings retained to compound growth, rather than paid out to shareholders as dividends.
■ Financial leverage—The ratio of assets to equity, which measures how much of a company's assets are financed by equity (rather than debt).
■ Asset turnover—The ratio of sales to total assets, which measures how efficiently a company generates sales.

The product of these four relationships has tracked earnings growth and stock market performance. The benefit of disaggregating earnings growth into these four factors is that one can fine-tune an outlook for future earnings growth. In the remaining years of this earnings cycle, I expect profit margins and the retention ratio to act as a drag on earnings growth and leverage and asset turnover to act as drivers of earnings growth.

Profit Margin

In general, the profit margin of a company is tied to the business cycle. As production rises, the costs of production are spread over a greater amount of output. This reduces the per-unit cost of output and raises the profit margin on each unit sold or service performed. As production slows, the opposite occurs. Thus, profit margins are highly cyclical.

During the 1990s earnings cycle, profit margins realized the longest period of expansion since the 1960s (see Figure 2.8). This was due, in part, to a lengthy business cycle, corporate restructurings in the early 1990s, and a return to the long-term trend rate of productivity growth. In aggregate, the profit margin for S&P 500 companies now stands near record highs. Profit margins may be maintained as capacity utilization

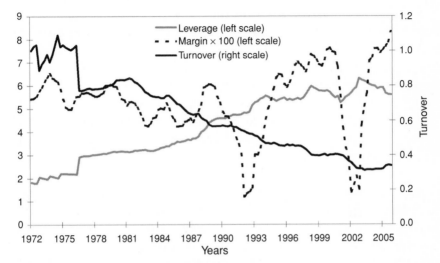

FIGURE 2.8 Drivers of earnings growth.
Components of return on equity for S&P 500 companies.

continues to rise. However, it is more likely that margins have peaked as a driver for this business cycle for two reasons:

■ First, margins rebounded sharply over the past few years. During that time, sales rose as the economy reaccelerated from recession. At the same time, expenses remained contained as companies spent little on hiring or investment. Profit margins have been the key driver of earnings over the past few years. However, there are signs that increasing hiring and inventory investment may soon put pressure on margins.

■ Second, as I previously mentioned, the artificial boost to profit margins from falling tax expense (pre-tax margins have not kept up with after-tax margins) is now fading and interest rates are likely to have bottomed near 40-year lows. This boost to profit margins from falling tax interest expenses has likely ended.

The rise and fall of profit margins magnify the trend in sales and help to define the saw-tooth pattern of the earnings cycle. Across earnings cycles, profit margins have remained close to their average level of 5.5 percent. Profit margins are likely to have peaked as a driver of earnings growth for this earnings cycle. I expect that the pattern of profit margins will remain cyclical and the trend will remain consistent across cycles.

Retention Ratio

The second component of earnings growth that is likely to contribute to a slower pace of earnings growth in the remaining years of this business cycle is the retention ratio—the percentage of earnings retained by a company to compound future growth. The retention ratio is the inverse of the dividend payout ratio, which is the percentage of earnings paid out to shareholders. Currently the dividend payout ratio stands around 30 percent, so the retention ratio is 70 percent.

Dividends per share grew in the early to mid-1960s, but then began to fall until the early 1970s. Through the mid-1970s, inflation soared and dividend yields had to compete with double-digit yields on Treasuries. Consequently, dividends-per-share rebounded. In the late 1970s and early 1980s, back-to-back recessions marked the beginning of a long secular downtrend in dividend growth. One of the primary drivers of this downtrend was the tax rate on dividend distributions, which compared unfavorably with falling capital gains rates, that encouraged business leaders to buy back stock as an alternative means to return value to shareholders (see Figure 2.9).

The 40-year decline in the dividend payout ratio appears to have bottomed because of a cyclical bounce back in profits, a shift in the taxation of dividends, and the perception of dividends as a form of capital discipline. (The reversal in the dividend payout ratio is discussed in more detail in Chapter 3.) The other side of the equation is that the retention ratio has likely peaked. A rise in the retention ratio acts as a drag on earnings growth.

Financial Leverage

The third component of earnings growth—and one likely to act as a positive for earnings-per-share growth—is financial leverage. Financial leverage relates to how a company is financed. The more debt supporting a company's assets, the more concentrated its net profits are in the hands of its shareholders.

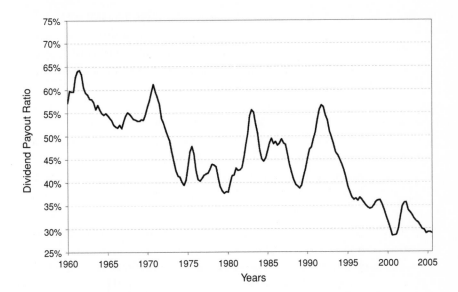

FIGURE 2.9   Dividend payout ratio.
Percent of operating earnings paid as dividend by S&P 500 companies.

Leverage has been steadily rising for the past 30 years, helping drive earnings-per-share growth (see Figure 2.8). In the 1990s, many companies issued debt to buy back stock. Shrinking the number of outstanding shares through stock buybacks increases earnings-per-share. Stock buybacks have continued in the current earnings cycle. In 2004 and 2005, they occurred at a strong, record-setting pace.

Although leverage is a positive for earnings growth, it will not likely be the primary driver of earnings growth because leverage is already relatively high. Financial leverage will, however, offer a small contribution to additional earnings growth.

Asset Turnover

The fourth component of earnings growth, asset turnover, has been steadily declining over the past 30 years. This key earnings driver is at the start of a new upward trend. In fact, rising asset turnover will likely be the primary driver of the 7 percent earnings growth for the companies in the S&P 500 for the remainder of the earnings cycle. To understand why, let's look back at why it declined.

Asset turnover is the ratio of sales to total assets. The higher the dollar amount of sales per dollar of assets used to create those sales, the higher the turnover ratio. Asset turnover varies across industries. Industries that require a substantial amount of assets in the form of plants and factories, like utilities and industrial manufacturing, have lower-than-average turnover ratios. Others industries, such as retailing, have above-average turnover ratios.

It seems logical that the overall asset turnover ratio for U.S. companies would have been steadily rising in recent decades. The composition of U.S. businesses has shifted away from manufacturing and other asset-heavy industries toward generally high-asset turnover service industries. In addition, the United States has experienced a resurgence in productivity—increasing output, or sales, relative to the assets employed to create the goods or services sold. Despite how logical a rise in asset turnover may seem, asset turnover has actually fallen steadily for decades (see Figure 2.8).

The reason asset turnover has fallen has more to do with assets than sales. U.S. corporations have been growing non-productive assets on their balance sheets at a pace many times faster than productivity. Intangible and other assets were only 4 percent of total assets 20 years ago. Today, they are more than 16 percent of total assets—a four fold increase. Merger and acquisition (M&A) deals that involved large premiums have been a major culprit because they place huge amounts of goodwill (an intangible asset) on balance sheets. These assets are not productive in a normal sense—they do not create any output. All too often, the brand value that intangible assets represent never pays off. Think of it as balance sheet "deadweight."

The addition of this deadweight has caused overall asset turnover to decline, even though the turnover of productive assets, such as property, plant, equipment (PPE), and inventory, has risen. The turnover of PPE and inventory has been rising steadily over the past 30 years (see Figure 2.10). Not surprisingly, it was the technology and telecommunications services sectors that experienced the biggest declines in asset turnover in the early 2000s, compared with the late 1990s, after record-breaking, high-premium mergers and acquisitions.

If high-premium merger and acquisition activity slows relative to sales growth, and disciplined business leaders are able to generate more revenue per dollar of assets, then asset turnover will likely reverse

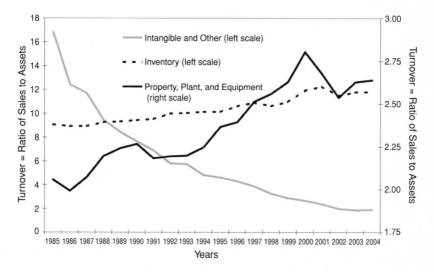

FIGURE 2.10   Turnover of productive assets have been rising while non-productive
has been falling.
Ratios of sales to assets by type of asset.

its long time downward trend. If asset turnover rises, it will become a
boost to earnings growth.

Corporate America does appear to have become more disciplined.
Corporate leaders have been more hesitant this business cycle to spend
on hiring, inventory, and capital improvements and additions. Even
more significantly, the premiums on merger and acquisition deals that
have taken place since the 2001 recession have been relatively low (see
Figure 2.11). Premiums have fallen to around 20 percent from the 40
percent to 60 percent averages of the past. The lower premiums reflect
the adaptation of business strategies to the evolving environment. Past
periods of heightened merger and acquisition activity resulted from
shocks to the business environment caused by shifts in competition,
regulation, inflation, technology, or globalization. These shifts help to
define the evolution current taking place. As a result, it appears that
another period of substantial M&A activity is beginning. I believe the
following factors are creating the current conditions that are conducive
to deals:

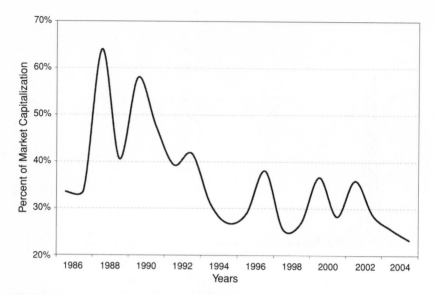

FIGURE 2.11   Announced merger & acquisition premiums.
Deal values expressed as % of total market capitalization.

■ An environment of slower economic growth, low capacity utilization, and constrained pricing power, which prompts business to grow
via acquisitions rather than increased capacity.
■ High corporate cash balances and low debt levels, which offer plenty
of fuel and capacity for deals.
■ Rising global competition from countries with low labor costs such
as China and India.
■ The expiration of the deadline for post-accounting scandal regulatory changes.

M&A activity has already demonstrated a powerful rebound. However, I believe that this wave of deals will be unique not only by being
the largest in history, but also by reflecting the lowest premiums. Asset
turnover will benefit from the consolidation and low premiums of the
emerging wave of M&A activity. See Figure 2.12.

Also, new processes and technologies focused on increasing asset
efficiency and squeezing more revenue per dollar of assets may be the
new killer applications. For example, a major national retailer is requiring that its suppliers use radio frequency identification (RFID). A few

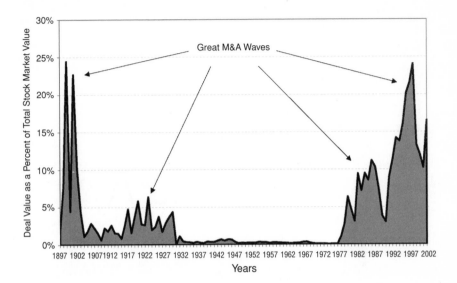

FIGURE 2.12   Merger and acquisition waves.
Merger & acquisition deal value as a percent of total stock market value.

high-profile technology manufacturers are also using RFID. For many types of companies, RFID tags on products enables real-time integration with suppliers to more effectively manage inventory assets. This type of advanced asset-tracking is enhancing operational efficiency. When companies optimize their supply chains, they can reduce the risk of supply shortages without holding excess raw materials. This is especially valuable for health care and manufacturing companies that use perishable supplies. Retailers stand to gain additional benefits from RFID, such as the potential elimination of traditional checkout areas and associated lines, as well as improved theft detection. The long-term implications of RFID are far reaching in terms of asset turnover.

Leaner, more focused U.S. businesses that can contain intangible asset growth and can use new technologies and processes should see a potentially powerful rebound in asset turnover. Asset turnover is arguably the most powerful component of the four key relationships that drive earnings growth.

During the past couple of years, investors focused on profit margins as they rocketed back from depressed levels—and rightfully so. But in today's environment of slower economic growth and peaking profit margins, it makes sense to pay more attention to asset turnover. The constituents of earnings growth are evolving. In the new era of investment performance, rising asset turnover is likely to be the primary driver of earnings-per-share growth for the companies in the S&P 500 as it reverses the downward trend of the last era.

Pulling It Together: Valuations and Earnings

My outlook for the two components of stock market price performance—the pace of earnings growth and the valuation the market is likely to assign to that growth—leads me to expect that stock market price performance will track earnings growth and average 7 percent over the next 10 years. Adding to that a 2 percent dividend yield, stock investors can expect a total return of 9 percent.

This modest investment performance may seem disappointing relative to the total returns for stocks since the 1920s and the even more generous returns in the 1990s. A total return of 9 percent suggests a new era of investment performance since 9 percent is below the past 80-years' average annual total return of 12.4 percent for stocks, and well below the average annual total return of 14.5 percent of the past 20 years. Total returns are likely to fall a few percentage points below the long-term average. Inflation will also remain below its long-term average of 4.5 percent. When adjusted for inflation, total returns will remain relatively consistent with those of the past. The same is also true for bonds. With a more muted outlook for inflation, the long-term trend in real investment gains will likely be preserved.

Since earnings cycles have consistently delivered earnings growth of around 7 percent, the disparity in stock market performance across cycles can be measured by changes in valuation. If the price-to-earnings ratio is expected to be relatively stable within a range of 14 to 22 times the level of earnings for the current earnings cycle, then valuations will not offer much of a magnifying effect. Therefore, the stock market is left to track the average 7 percent pace of earnings growth.

Earnings and stock prices have had a very tight historical relationship with a high long-term correlation. Could this be changing? Could investors begin to look beyond earnings as an underlying driver of investor return? The next chapter explores this.

CHAPTER 3

The Dividend Revolution

Dividends seem to get the least respect of the three components of stock market total return. In this chapter, I seek to elevate the relative standing of dividends.

- Dividends as a percentage of an investor's total return in the stock market have fallen dramatically during the past 25 years, from the 40 percent to 50 percent range to an average of just 14 percent over the past ten years. I expect a reversal of the long downward trend in the new era of investment performance.
- As conditions have evolved, the key drivers of the long-term downtrend in dividends have been eliminated or reversed. Dividend issuance has started to make a comeback.
- I predict the growth in dividends per share will exceed earnings per share over the next ten years. Dividends are likely to become a much more important component of stock market total return than over the past ten years.

The bear market associated with the Great Depression in the 1930s and the long bear market of the 1970s resulted in ten-year periods during which all of the return on stocks came from dividends. I do not expect this to repeat but I do expect that, over the long-term, dividends are likely to make up 20 percent or more of stock total return, an increase from the 14 percent average of the past ten years. The last time dividends consistently accounted for 20 percent to 30 percent of total return was the 1960s. See Figure 3.1.

Dividends are likely to make up a rising percentage of stock market total return, not only because of faster dividend growth, but also because of slower price appreciation for stocks than in the prior two decades, as detailed in Chapters 1 and 2. Without the benefit of price-to-earnings multiple expansion, stock market total returns will be driven by earnings growth and dividend yield. In this new era of investment performance, price performance should track the 70-year trend in profit growth of 7 percent and dividends should contribute a 2 percent yield, generating a 9 percent annualized total return for the stock market for next ten years.

The dividend yield for U.S. companies has been trending lower for many decades. The only exceptions to this secular trend were the inflation spikes in the 1940s and 1970s, when dividend yields were forced to compete with soaring bond yields. Although the dividend yield for the S&P 500 companies averaged 5 percent from 1926 (when the S&P

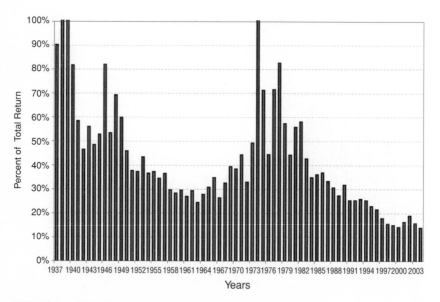

FIGURE 3.1   Dividend portion of stock market total return.
10-year average of S&P 500 dividend as a percent of total return.

500 was established) through 1980, it has fallen below 2 percent in recent years. Dividends per share grew in the early- to mid-1960s, but then began to fall until the early 1970s. Through the mid-1970s, dividends per share rebounded; as inflation soared, U.S. Treasury securities were offering double-digit yields. The back-to-back recessions of the late 1970s and early 1980s marked the beginning of a long secular downtrend in dividend growth. Dividend yields remain very low, but the dividend-per-share growth appears to be beginning to rebound. Some of the drivers of the long downtrend are beginning to reverse. See Figure 3.2.

Taxes were a key driver of the downtrend in dividend payouts. Historically, income was taxed at a higher rate than capital gains and, for individuals, dividends were taxed as income. As the capital gains tax rate fell, stock buybacks became a more tax efficient means to return value to shareholders. Decades ago, high-income investors faced federal taxes on dividends of up to 91 percent. In 2003, Congress passed dividend-tax-relief legislation that cut the top tax rate to 15 percent on

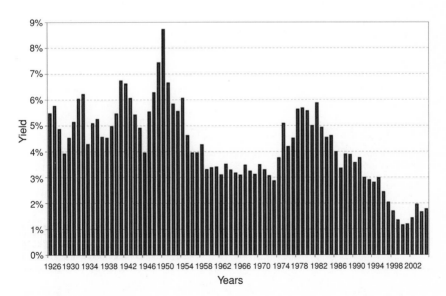

FIGURE 3.2   Dividend yields have fallen well below the long-term average.
S&P 500 dividend yield.

most dividends. With the tax rate on long-term capital gains at 15 percent, both dividends and capital gains are now taxed at the same rate, eliminating the bias toward buying back stock from investors over dividends as a way to return value to shareholders. See Figure 3.3.

Dividends are no guarantee of good corporate governance. However, unlike earnings, dividends cannot be later restated or written off. Therefore, they appear to reflect greater transparency and capital discipline. After record numbers of write-offs in 2002 that reflected wasted capital, investors may be ready to afford a higher share price to those companies offering a dividend.

With the cost of borrowing likely to remain low relative to history, the benefit of retaining earnings to finance future growth rather than paying them out to shareholders is also low. Additionally, the greater percentage of retained earnings in the 1990s (the retention ratio rose to 71 percent and the dividend payout ratio fell to 29 percent) failed to deliver superior earnings growth when compared to prior cycles during which a greater portion of earnings was paid out to shareholders.

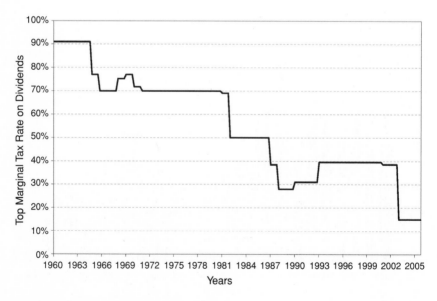

FIGURE 3.3   Taxes on dividends have fallen.
Top marginal dividend tax rate.

The S&P 500 currently offers a dividend yield of around 2 percent. For the first time in more than a decade, the percentage of companies in the S&P 500 that pay dividends rose meaningfully in 2003 (see figure 3.4). As the number of companies paying dividends in the index rises, the dividend yield will rise and compound the rising payout ratios of those companies already paying dividends. Indeed, this is already taking place. More than 300 of the companies in the S&P 500 increased their dividend-per-share payout in 2005—a 16 percent increase over 2004.

DPS versus EPS

Although 2003 marked the turnaround in companies paying dividends, the performance of dividend-paying stocks lagged the market in 2003. It was not until 2005 that the stocks of companies in the S&P 500 that pay dividends appeared to bottom versus the stocks of non-payers (see

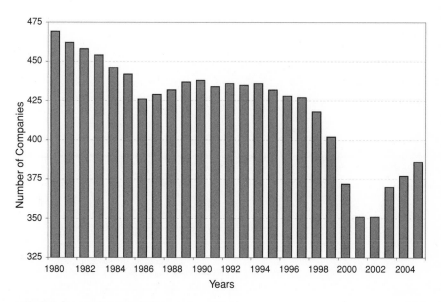

FIGURE 3.4 Dividends are coming back.
Number of S&P 500 companies that pay a dividend.

Figure 3.5). This is in contrast to the average out-performance by non-payers during the prior ten years. Why did it take until 2005 for dividends to begin to matter to investors? The most likely reason was that earnings-per-share (EPS) growth, which was stronger than dividend-per-share (DPS) growth, drove stock prices higher.

In 2005, DPS growth rose at a mid-teens pace, exceeding EPS growth for the first time during this earnings cycle. This was, finally, the catalyst needed for investors to refocus their investment decision-making on dividends. Is this the beginning of a new trend in the years to come? I think so, for several reasons:

- The annual dividend-per-share growth for companies in the S&P 500 is likely to average 10 percent over the next ten years, compared with earnings growth of just 7 percent, as dividend payout ratio climbs back toward the long-term average.

- U.S. corporations are subject to a recently imposed accounting rule requiring the expensing of employee stock options. In response,

FIGURE 3.5   Performance of dividend payers has bottomed.
Relative performance of S&P 500 stocks that are dividend payers versus non-dividend payers.

many companies have recently changed their compensation structures by granting shares, rather than options, to key employees. One result of this change is that management compensation—once linked solely to stock price—becomes directly linked to stock price and dividends. Dividend policy may become an even more prominent component of corporate strategy.

■ Many companies, even those in historically low-dividend-yielding sectors, have recently introduced a dividend or have meaningfully increased their dividend, enabling investors to value more stocks on the basis of dividends.

In short, dividends have begun to make a comeback. The growth rate of dividends has recently surged to highs not seen since the late 1970s (see Figure 3.6). Although the dividend yield remains low on a pre-tax basis, they are near their long-term average on an after-tax basis,

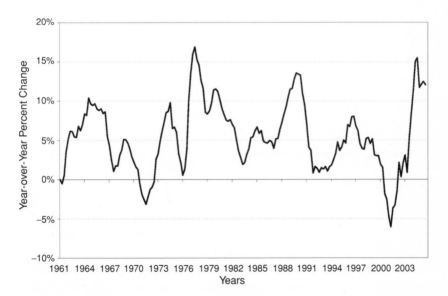

FIGURE 3.6   Dividends per share are growing at the strongest pace since the late 1980s.
S&P 500 dividend per share year-over-year growth rate.

given the new lower dividend tax rate. During the next ten years, dividend yields may reach 2 percent on an after-tax basis, which is near the top of the historical range. See Figure 3.7.

How will companies fund increased dividend payments? By reversing the trend of the past 20 years and shifting a portion of the funds used for stock buybacks to dividends. The companies that make up the S&P 500 currently spend more on stock buybacks than on dividends. Buybacks, or repurchases of outstanding shares by corporations, have soared relative to dividends since 1982, when the Securities and Exchange Commission gave companies the ability to repurchase shares without incurring liability for manipulating their stock price (if done in accordance with applicable requirements). Interestingly, as buybacks replaced dividends as the preferred form of returning capital to shareholders, the total payout to shareholders (combining both share buybacks and dividends) stayed relatively constant as a percentage of earnings (see Figure 3.8). Now that the drivers that supported buybacks have reversed, it makes sense that the pendulum would swing back in favor of dividends over buybacks.

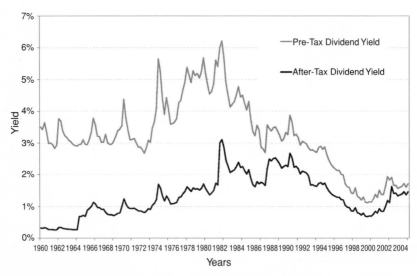

FIGURE 3.7   After-tax dividend yield is near historical average.
Pre-tax and after-tax dividend yield assuming top marginal dividend tax rate.

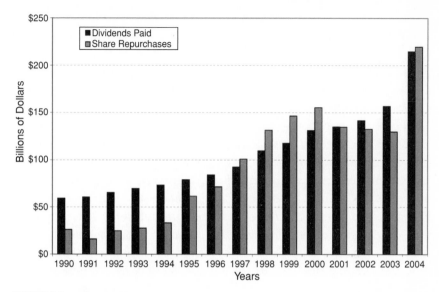

FIGURE 3.8   Cash payments to investors.
S&P 500 buybacks and dividends (billions of $).

Tying It Together

I expect a rebound from the 40-year decline in the dividend payout ratio. In fact, the ratio could go to 40 percent by the end of the decade, from today's 29 percent. What could produce such a dramatic shift? A dividend growth rate of around 10 percent, which is well above the average growth rates of the past two decades, and well above the 7 percent pace of earnings growth projected for the next ten years.

The biggest risk to this thesis—the return of the dividend—may be the outlook for tax rates. The dividend tax rate is set to go from 15 percent to 39.6 percent around the end of the decade, barring an extension of the 2003 tax cuts. Much of the outlook for taxes may depend on the status of the federal budget as the expiration of the 2003 cuts nears.

Valuing Dividends

A renewed interest in dividends may have a significantly positive effect on the value of the stock market. In theory, the price of a share of stock is today's value of all future cash flows that accrue to that share—meaning dividends. However, as companies shifted emphasis away from dividends, investors used earnings to represent these cash flows. This has been reflected in stock market prices, which have tended to move in line with earnings in recent decades. However, a renewed focus on dividends may result in valuations that are based more on the prospects for the actual cash flows of dividends.

Moreover, the entire stock market now can be valued on the basis of dividends. Many companies, even those in historically low-dividend-yielding sectors such as information technology, recently have introduced a dividend or have meaningfully increased their dividend. For example, five years ago only two of the current top-ten semiconductor firms paid dividends, now only two of them do not. The growth rate of dividends in the information technology sector has topped all other sectors, allowing the stock market as a whole to be valued on the basis of dividends.

Our base case outlook for the financial markets includes an annual dividend growth rate of 10 percent, which would result in a 40 percent dividend payout ratio in ten years. If investors focus on the faster growth rate of dividends, rather than earnings, higher valuations may result. Using a compounded 10 percent growth rate for cash flows rather than 7 percent over the next ten years produces a difference in the value of the stock market of more than 30 percent! I believe that the most likely scenario is for stock prices to track 7 percent earnings growth and dividend yields to rise to 2 percent. However, the potential for stronger *price* returns related to faster dividend growth is not out of the question.

In fact, the stock market could see a valuation spike if investors shift their focus to dividends. Given my assumptions for interest rates and risk premiums, the S&P 500 could appreciate even more dramatically if investors price in a dividend growth rate of 13 percent. Is this a realistic estimate? Although our base case estimate is 10 percent, 13 percent seems within reason. A 13 percent annual dividend growth rate would lead to a dividend payout ratio of 54 percent in ten years, which happens to be the average since the S&P 500 index was established in 1926.

CHAPTER 4

Back to the Future

Mark Twain once said, "History does not repeat itself. But it does rhyme." The prior three chapters examined not only what to expect in the new era of investment performance, but also provided the historical perspective on the evolutionary path of each of the key drivers of investment return.

History is important, but context is everything when it comes to evaluating market behavior. Finding the right historical comparison, rather than a simple historical average, can yield far superior results when forecasting. A comparable period in the past isn't likely to be a blueprint of the future, but instead provides a test of the proposed relationships between factors that influence market behavior.

Is History Repeating Itself?

Looking back to find a comparable period in history to the likely environment of the coming years, the 1960s stand out as a period that rhymes nicely. During the decade of the 1960s, the annual total return on the stock market was 9 percent and the average bond market total return was 4 percent. This is a close and rare match with what is envisioned in the years ahead for these two major classes of investments. However, it is not enough simply to look at returns. It is also important to look at the drivers of those returns.

John Maynard Keynes, an exceptional investor and one of the fathers of macroeconomics, warned that, "It is dangerous to apply to

53

the future inductive arguments based on past experience, unless one can distinguish the broad reasons why past experience was what it was." The 1960s were what they were because of key drivers like interest rates, inflation, productivity, profits and valuations—in addition to economic, regulatory, and geopolitical factors. In these drivers there are also similarities to what I foresee in the coming years.

■ Interest rates, measured by the yield on the ten-year Treasury, averaged 4.9 percent in the 1960s close to the 4.7 percent so far this decade.
■ Productivity growth averaged an annualized 2.8 percent back then, near my 2.5 percent expectation for the next ten years.
■ Inflation averaged a subdued annualized 2.3 percent, which is within the 2–3 percent range forecast for the next ten years.
■ Earnings grew at 8 percent in the 1960s, as compared to my forecast of 7 percent for this decade.
■ P/E multiples averaged 18, within a relatively flat and narrow range of 14 to 22 (see Figure 4.1).
■ Operating profits recently rose to over 10 percent of GDP; profits exceeded 10 percent of GDP from late 1961 to early 1969, after which they went into steep decline.
■ Fiscal and trade imbalances were growing due to a rising budget deficit and the growth of Japan into a global economic power.

The most recent recession ended in November 2001. February 1961 marked the end of a recession. The expansion of the 1960s was one of the longest on record, lasting until December 1969, when a relatively mild recession occurred.

Less than two years after the end of the recessions in 1961 and 2001, a global conflict over weapons of mass destruction ensued (Cuban missile crisis then, Iraq now) as part of a larger ideological war (Cold War, terrorism). Comparing 1962–1963 with 2002–2003, we can see the depth of the parallels between the two eras (see Figure 4.2). From a geopolitical perspective:

■ The Cuban missile crisis was arguably the most dangerous period of the Cold War. The United States uncovered evidence of Soviet missiles

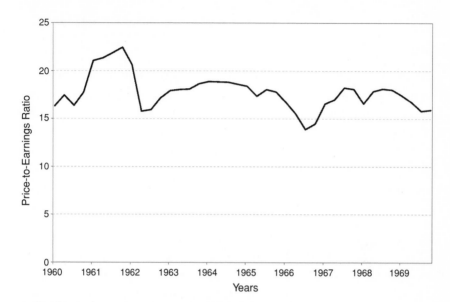

FIGURE 4.1   Stock market valuation in 1960s.
S&P 500 price-to-earnings ratio on prior four quarters earnings.

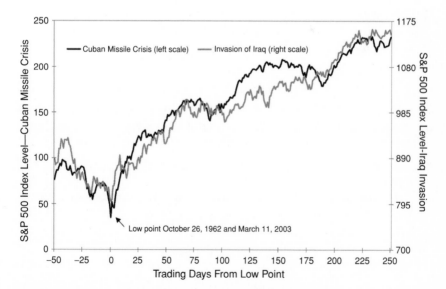

FIGURE 4.2   Stock market performance surrounding geopolitical events.
S&P 500 Index surrounding Cuban missile crisis and Iraq invasion.

in Cuba capable of delivering nuclear warheads anywhere in the
United States. In late 1962, Canada proposed that eight neutral nations
be chosen to make on-site UN inspections of weapon sites in Cuba.
The UN weapons inspection teams that entered Iraq in late 2002
seemed to mirror that effort. Despite the geopolitical tension, as the
United States took action with a military blockade of Cuba in October
of 1962, the stock market rallied. The stock market reacted similarly
in the days leading up to the invasion of Iraq, in March of 2003.

- The war on terror in Afghanistan was another regional conflict brew-
  ing in 2002–03; in 1962–63 the United States deployed military per-
  sonnel to Vietnam.
- In 1962, North Korea set up an Atomic Energy Center to develop
  nuclear weapons and by 1963 its first reactor was under construction. In 2002, North Korea announced it would resume construction
  of reactors and uranium enrichment processes and, in 2003, formally
  announced a withdrawal from the Nuclear Non-Proliferation Treaty.
- Terrorist attacks were taking place around the world during both
  periods.

Beyond the geopolitical similarities, the 1962–63 and the 2002–03
periods exhibited a similar economic, fiscal, monetary, market, profit,
and regulatory backdrop for the financial markets.

- In both 1963 and 2003, the sitting President focused his State of the
  Union address on a program of tax cuts to stimulate the economy
  and reduce unemployment heading into the third year of his term.
  During both years, Congress enacted tax cuts and the unemploy-
  ment rate fell from over 6 percent to around 5 percent by year end.
- The federal budget was moving back into deficit from a period of
  surplus.
- The Federal Reserve was pumping liquidity into the financial system.
- The ten-year Treasury Note yield was close to 4 percent and the
  pace of inflation was around 1 to 2 percent.
- Productivity growth was almost identical during both periods, at 3
  percent.
- Economic growth was robust in both periods.
- Earnings growth for the companies in the S&P 500 averaged in the
  mid-single digits.

- Stock market valuation, measured by the price-to-earnings ratio on the prior four quarters of earnings, stood around 19.
- In 1963, the S&P 500 provided a total return around 23 percent, similar to the 29 percent in 2003.
- Investor mistrust was heightened as the Securities and Exchange Commission conducted lengthy investigations into "abuses" by securities firms.

Rhymes with the 60s?

Clearly, the outlook for investment performance presented in the earlier chapters has a precedent in the 1960s and a tight parallel period in the years that followed the 1961 and 2001 recessions. Will the next ten years be a repeat of the environment and investment performance witnessed from 1966 to 1976? Probably not, although it may rhyme. The next five years may be similar to the late 1960s.

- The current economic cycle that began in 2001 may peak around the turn of the decade, as it did in December of 1969.
- The pattern of earnings growth is likely to follow the similar sawtooth pattern with a mid-cycle pause occurring in 2007, as it did in 1967.
- Valuations are likely to be similar to those of the second half of the 1960s, ranging from 14–19. Valuations, measured by the S&P 500 price-to-earnings ratio, ranged from 14–22 in the 1960s overall. However, in the later half of that decade, they moved within a tighter range of 14–19.
- Interest rates and inflation are likely to be higher in the second half of this decade than the first.

Despite the similarities with the 1960s, the series of challenges that plagued the U.S. economy in the early 1970s are unlikely to be repeated. Inflation began to rise unexpectedly as the 1960s ended, setting the stage for an economically volatile decade that was magnified by the effects of the 1973 Arab oil embargo. The early 1970s marked the worst recession and bear market for stocks since the Great Depression in the 1930s.

It is unlikely that a repeat of the soaring inflation and investment environment of the late 1960s and early 1970s is in store for the finan-

cial markets, as presented in Chapter 1. Nevertheless, the next ten years
pose challenges that are likely to lead to below-average investment performance. The coming years offer investors a different set of risks—the
unpredictable nature of severe weather, high energy prices, opaque
derivative markets, and demographic trends. These conditions are more
likely to rhyme with the 1960s than lead to a repeat of them.

Severe Weather Activity

In the 1960s, six major hurricanes made landfall in the U.S.—more than
in any decade since. Included among these was a category five hurricane named Camille, which did billions of dollars in damage to
Louisiana and Mississippi. It is tempting to assume away weather-
related events as non-forecastable and random. Nevertheless, weather
patterns have exerted a significant impact on the economy and profits
in the past. Experts are forecasting above-normal severe weather patterns characterized by substantially more major hurricanes over the next
ten years. The potential for a prolonged period of above-average severe
weather activity is a risk that could result in:

- Lost economic output.
- Downgrades to municipal debt ratings as emergency reserve funds
  are depleted.
- Higher agriculture prices.
- A rise in unemployment in affected areas.
- A negative impact on insurance company reserves and profits.
- Higher Energy prices.

The economic implications of a prolonged period of severe weather
activity for the insurance industry are distressing. According to the
Department of Energy, insurance losses from natural disasters have
increased 15-fold since 1960, adjusted for inflation. In 1992, Hurricane
Andrew cost approximately $22 billion (in today's dollars) in insured
losses and was the second most costly hurricane in terms of insured
damages. Seven insurance companies went bankrupt after that severe
weather event. Estimates for Hurricane Katrina from the insurance
industry have reached approximately $60 billion in insured losses. In
total, Katrina could cost the Gulf Coast states as much as an additional
$120 billion. While the insurance industry appears in better shape today

than it was in the early 1990s, insurers are unlikely to have adequate reserves if major hurricanes causing tens of billions of dollars increase to annual frequency.

As Katrina illustrated, energy prices can be affected dramatically by severe weather. It is possible that a weather-related risk premium eventually becomes embedded in domestic energy prices if severe storm activity begins to affect supplies with increased regularity. Energy products that come to the United States from politically unstable or terrorist-threatened parts of the world already contain risk premiums in their pricing. The four back-to-back hurricanes that hit the southern United States in the summer of 2004 resulted in a loss of 25 percent of Gulf of Mexico energy production for a period of time. In the summer and fall of 2005, Hurricane Katrina shut down over 60 percent of production in the Gulf.

High Energy Prices

On October 16, 1973, OPEC cut oil production and placed an embargo on shipments of crude oil to the West. The effects of the embargo were immediate. Not only did prices rise as supply pulled back, but shortages were common. The price of oil quadrupled by 1974 to nearly $12 per barrel. While energy prices are high and unlikely to return to the long-term average of around $18 per barrel, that kind of supply shock is not likely to be repeated.

Why? Primarily because the Earth is not running out of oil, contrary to doomsday-type predictions.

- Proven oil reserves have grown faster than oil consumption during the past ten years.
- At a price of $30 (US) per barrel or higher, oil is economical to extract in vast quantities from non-conventional sources.
- U.S. investment in oilfield and mining equipment has risen to a record high, as did the worldwide number of oil rigs in operation.
- Oil demand growth during the past five years has been in line with the 35-year average.
- Inventories of energy commodities are at or above five-year average levels as production has kept up with consumption. See Figure 4.3.

Nevertheless, Americans have been fearful of energy shortages since the gasoline-rationing days of the early 1970s. Our fears, however, may be unfounded. At the end of 2003, the world's proven crude oil reserves were 12 percent higher than levels a decade ago and equal to about 40 years of consumption at current rates. This fact has been highlighted by former Fed chairman Alan Greenspan:

> *Increasingly sophisticated techniques have facilitated far deeper drilling of promising fields, especially offshore, and have significantly increased the average proportion of oil reserves eventually brought to the surface. During the past decade, despite more than 250 billion barrels of oil extracted worldwide, net proved reserves rose in excess of 100 billion barrels. That is, gross additions to reserves have significantly exceeded the extraction of oil the reserves replaced. Indeed, in fields where, two decades ago, roughly one-third of the oil in place ultimately could be extracted, almost half appears to be recoverable today. I exclude from these calculations the reported vast reserves of so-called unconventional oils such as Canadian tar sands and Venezuelan heavy oil.*

> —Former Federal Reserve Chairman Alan Greenspan, in a speech to the National Italian American Foundation, October 15, 2004.

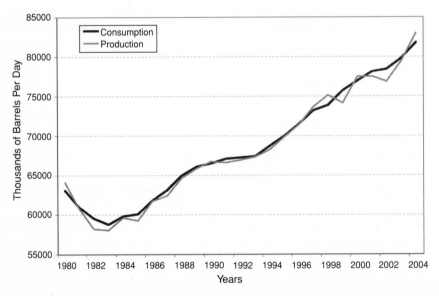

FIGURE 4.3   World oil production and consumption.
U.S. Department of Energy Global Production and Consumption.

The Canadian oil sands are worth including in the analysis. The United States already imports more petroleum from Canada than from Saudi Arabia—in fact, we import more petroleum from Canada than from any other country. The Canadian oil sands contain 1.6 trillion barrels of oil—this one source alone could meet the global demand for oil for over 50 years.

In contrast to traditional, expensive oil exploration, the cost of finding this oil source in Canada is effectively zero. On the other hand, the costs of extracting oil from oil sand is much higher than pumping it from an oil field—some analysts estimate that sand extraction costs $10 to $15 per barrel versus just under $5 for more traditional means. For years, this cost differential had prohibited large-scale oil production from the Canadian sands. However, at an average oil price of $30 per barrel, the oil sands projects in Canada have the potential to generate a 15 percent rate of return—enough to attract the interest of major oil companies and enough to make it viable to produce vast amounts of oil over the long-term. In fact, as oil prices rose in 2004, Shell and Chevron-Texaco jointly opened the $5.7 billion Athabasca Oil Sands Project in Alberta, Canada, which is on track to increase production to 500,000 barrels of oil per day.

Venezuela's Orinoco Belt, another non-conventional source of vast amounts of oil that are economical to extract, currently yields 500,000 barrels daily and that number should spike higher as new operations open there.

According to the International Energy Agency, global oil demand has grown at a 1.8 percent annual pace since 1970. It continues to average this pace, growing 1.4 percent in 2005 and is expected to grow 2.2 percent in 2006. These estimates include rapid demand growth from China and India. China makes up about 2 percent of total world oil imports. However, it is very important to note that rapid oil-demand growth by emerging nations has been offset by greater energy efficiency in the developed world. As illustrated in Chapter 1, thirty years ago the U.S. required nearly one and a half barrels of oil to produce each $1,000 of total national output, measured by Gross Domestic Product (GDP). Today, our larger and more information-oriented economy consumes a little more than a half of a barrel of oil to produce $1,000 of GDP, or just over one-third as much as we used to.

The long-term historical average price for a barrel of crude oil has been $18. The long-term equilibrium price is more likely double the long-term average, or somewhere around $40 per barrel (with risk of even higher prices) due to a number of factors:

■ More expensive sources of oil are needed to meet the steady 1.8 percent annual rise in demand. Tapping the vast quantities of oil available from the Canadian oil sands and Venezuelan heavy-oil sources takes time and is considerably more expensive than conventional sources.

■ Much of the world's oil supply meeting today's demand is in regions that are currently fraught with heightened terrorism risk and geopolitical instability, which results in a event-risk premium imbedded in the price of oil.

■ A weaker U.S. dollar may allow the dollar-denominated price of oil to drift higher than it otherwise might.

■ OPEC may perceive that they have more power to raise oil prices. Demand did not weaken until market prices rose well above OPEC's own stated target range.

Tapping the vast quantities of oil available from Canadian oil sands and Venezuelan heavy oil sources takes time, even now that the major oil companies feel more assured that higher-than-long-term average prices are here to stay. Until then, OPEC is the marginal producer of oil.

According to a January 2005 report by the International Energy Agency, 75 percent of OPEC's current spare capacity is concentrated in Saudi Arabia, enabling that country to be the principal voice within the cartel. Historically, the dominance of the Saudis' excess capacity has bolstered their strength within OPEC, a position that favored lower prices, at least externally. If, over time, Saudi Arabia's role in setting production policy lessens due to capacity increases elsewhere in the cartel, then the price-setting process will become more democratic and likely lead to a higher acceptable-price band. As long as demand remains supportive and spare capacity is tight, OPEC may maintain an average price of at least double the long-term average of $18 in the coming years.

Higher prices for energy commodities are distressing to us all. But should they invoke a comparison to the shortage-plagued 1970s? No. This time the rise in prices is not the result of a supply shock (a sudden cutback in supply). Therefore, the impact on growth is much more benign. Because the driver of the current rise in prices has been steady demand growth, rather than the sudden drop in supply, the outcome is likely to be different than it was in the 1970s. The sudden cutback in the availability of oil in the 1970s had dire consequences for the U.S. economy. Those willing to pay much higher prices often found there was none to buy. Presently, oil is available to those willing to pay higher prices. And, even more importantly, the economy is much less dependent on energy commodities for fueling economic growth.

As consumers and businesses adjust their demand in light of higher prices, the pace of economic growth may gradually slow more than it might have otherwise. However, higher energy costs are unlikely to cause a repeat of the deep downturn in the economy that took place in the early 1970s.

Derivatives

The credit-default swap market has grown tremendously in recent years. Credit-default swaps allow the banking system to transfer credit risk to less-leveraged investors, such as insurance companies and pension funds. Credit derivatives were a key reason the financial system weathered the largest bankruptcies in history—WorldCom and Enron—with no impairment of banks' capacity to lend. As a result, credit-default swaps have helped bring down the cost of borrowing.

However, there may be a dark side to credit-default swaps. Many new, less-creditworthy players jumped into the market eager to cash in by selling protection while the credit cycle was improving. The booming market for credit derivatives is so opaque that participants and regulators are often unsure which party actually ends up responsible in defaults on commercial bank loans and big lease contracts.

While market discipline is meant to keep risks in balance within the over-the-counter (OTC) market, a fundamental precondition for effective market discipline is transparency—a characteristic not found in the OTC marketplace. The risk is that at the end of this credit cycle credit protection may unravel as some entities default and others are left pointing fingers at each other. If that happens, some financial intermediaries may find themselves with unexpected default liability that may bring about a premature end to the business cycle.

The credit-default swap market is very broad. In contrast, the market for interest-rate swaps (where participants buy or sell interest-rate risk) is very narrow and, at the same time, very large. The $160 trillion dollar-derivatives market is dominated by the OTC interest-rate swaps and options market, making up more than 75 percent of the overall derivatives market. To put the size of this market in perspective, the total global bond market has a market value of $22.5 trillion.

The exchange-traded market for derivatives is small, transparent, and regulated. In contrast, the OTC market is only indirectly regulated, much less transparent, and has no formal limits on individual positions, leverage, or margin. The vast majority of activity in this market takes place through just a handful of dealers.

Dealers attempt to dynamically hedge risk by buying Treasuries when rates are falling and selling them when rates are rising, much like owners of mortgage bonds. This behavior led to the stock market crash of 1987. The dynamic hedging of derivative exposures led dealers to sell stocks in response to the drop in the stock market, which led to a further decline in stock prices and more selling by dealers in an accelerating feedback loop that created a dislocation in market liquidity—the result was the crash. Program trading collars and so-called "circuit breakers" on the stock market exchanges remain in place today as a legacy of the painful lesson learned on Black Monday in 1987.

While the impact of mortgage-backed bond investors on interest-rate volatility is an often-cited concern, the risk posed by the structure of the OTC interest-rate derivatives market may present a greater influence on interest-rate moves, exacerbating losses in the bond market.

In summary, both the market for credit default swaps and OTC interest rate swaps pose risks to financial markets that could materialize in the coming years.

Demographics

In contrast to the demographic profile of the 1960s and early 1970s when the workforce experienced an influx of younger workers, today the workforce is aging. The reason for this is the Baby Boom, a demographic wave in the United States between 1946 and 1964. Live births climbed from less than 3 million in 1946 to 4 million in 1954, then stayed above 4 million per year for eleven years. After 1964, the United States did not see 4 million births again in a single year until 1989, when Boomers themselves were having children. See Figure 4.4.

The oldest of the Boomers, those born in 1946, entered the workforce in the 1960s and are now old enough to be eligible to make withdrawals from retirement plans without penalty. However, it is unlikely that the Baby Boomers will begin retiring en masse and selling their investments to support themselves. The peak year for Baby Boom births was 1957, which means that while the oldest Boomers are now 60, most are still in their 40s. Most of the Baby Boom generation will be saving and investing for retirement during the next ten years. Their children— the Echo Boom, a cohort even larger than their parents—are now entering their working years and beginning to save and invest, too.

While not entailing dire circumstances for the financial markets, the demographic changes do have market impacts. One of the effects may be a rise in the saving rate and the demand for savings vehicles like stocks and bonds. On average, U.S. workers currently save less than 1 percent of their income—this is down from 6 percent ten years ago.

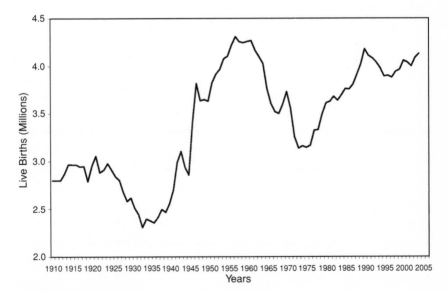

FIGURE 4.4   Live births.
U.S. Census Bureau, U.S. live births annually in millions.

One of the main reasons is that net worth grew very rapidly. At first, this was due to the strong performance of the stock market in the late 1990s. Then, the rise in home values in the 2000s allowed homeowners to feel wealthier because they could easily tap the rising equity in their home if they wanted or needed. While their net worth was growing very rapidly, workers did not feel the need to sacrifice and forego current consumption in order to save a few percent a year. However, as the growth in net worth slows over the next ten years, workers are likely again to save at higher rates. This should provide support for valuations of both stocks and bonds.

Another effect may be an increase in the demand for yield-producing investments. As the Boomers approach retirement, they may begin to favor investments that provide a steady stream of income. This may result in increasing demand for bonds and high-yielding stocks.

Although likely to live and work longer than their parents, the Boomers will eventually retire. The impact on savings may gradually begin to change 10 to 15 years from now. At first, the older Boomers will begin selling some of their holdings, but the large number of younger Boomers who are still investing will absorb the sales. Eventually, the Boomers will become net sellers. The Echo Boomers will absorb some of the supply as they save for their own retirement and they will have the help of the potentially larger market of investors from overseas. Many countries, particularly emerging market nations, have a demographic profile that is the opposite of developed nations like the U.S., providing demand for savings. If not, the alternative could be a structural bear market that could last throughout much of the second quarter of the 21st century.

Rhyming with History

The outlook for investment performance presented in the earlier chapters has a precedent in the 1960s, following a tight parallel period in the years that followed the 1961 and 2001 recessions. While not repeating the past, the next ten years will most likely rhyme with the late 1960s, but avoid the conditions that led to the dismal financial and economic performance of the early 1970s.

CHAPTER 5

Return and Volatility Forecasts

The earlier chapters presented a ten-year total return forecast for stocks (9 percent) and bonds (5 percent). This chapter provides details on both return and volatility forecasts by sub-category of stocks and bonds for the remainder of the business cycle, expected to last another three to six years. It also provides return and volatility forecasts for the next ten years to cover the transition into the next cycle. The most important thing to remember is that in this new era of investment performance, below-average returns are likely for most asset classes.

Why a Range?

I have specified return forecasts over a three-to-six-year time horizon within a range. There are a number of reasons why a range is preferable to a point estimate.

First, a point estimate provides a false sense of accuracy. My forecast ranges are narrow (7–9 percent for stocks) with just +/− 1 percent around the center point. To put this in perspective, it is very rare that the market has ever returned within +/− 1 percent of the long-term average in a year. In fact, only three times in the 78 year history of the S&P 500 did this happen. The index's performance in recent years, including the 26 percent gain in 2003, moved the long-term average return by nearly half a percentage point over a 77-year period! This shows that when forecasting over a ten or 20-year timeframe, the typical range of performance of the market over the course of a month could change that forecast by 1 percent or more. A more narrowly defined estimate of return simply is not useful in a practical sense.

Second, a point estimate provides a false confidence in the outcome and can lead to a fragile portfolio structure. A range is more appropriate for the strategic portfolio construction that I present in Part 2 of this book, which is designed to be optimal under a range of ways the future may unfold, and not just one potential future course of events. This allows for a robust portfolio structure that is more likely to meet one's objectives under a variety of circumstances. Why? By incorporating some adaptability into the portfolio structure, investors avoid being leveraged entirely to only one set of assumptions and gain a higher probability of achieving investment objectives. A strategic portfolio will not need constant tactical adjustments when the market moves, as would be implied by a portfolio constructed on single-point estimates of asset class rate of return and volatility.

And third, market returns tend not be normally distributed, which suggests that a range of volatility estimates is far more appropriate than a point estimate in describing our outlook for volatility.

As a result, I forecast a realistic range that I believe will reflect performance over the next 3–6 years. See Table 5.1.

TABLE 5.1   Total Return and Volatility Averages for Remainder of Business Cycle (3-6 Years)

Asset Class	Return	Volatility
Large-Cap Stocks	7–9%	14–18%
Mid-Cap Stocks	5–7%	15–20%
Small-Cap Stocks	4–6%	17–23%
International Stocks	8–10%	14–18%
Core Taxable Bonds	4–6%	4–6%
Short-Term Bonds	3–5%	1–3%
Long-Term Bonds	4–6%	7–11%
High-Yield Bonds	4–6%	7–11%
International Bonds	6–8%	8–11%
Municipal Bonds	3–5%	4–6%
Cash	3%	1%

Why Forecast Volatility?

We often talk about risk in terms of specific qualitative factors. However, in the financial markets, risk is most often defined by quantitative measures. Quantitative risk—measured by security price fluctuations—or volatility, is very important to understanding the path the markets may take. Understanding risk is very important; risk and return go hand-in-hand.

Volatility (measured by annual standard deviation) is likely to rise from current low levels for the remainder of this business cycle. Price volatility typically reflects investor uncertainty. Rising price volatility matters because it feeds investor uncertainty as the business cycle matures and creates opportunities to benefit from an adaptive portfolio structure through shifting the allocation to take advantage of mispricings.

Volatility for both the stock and bond markets is tied to the business cycle. Volatility tends to fall for both stocks and bonds as the economy is recovering from a recession and often rises as the business cycle matures. Shocks to financial markets, like the 1987 stock market crash or the 1998 Russian debt default, can result in temporary deviations from the cyclical pattern of volatility. Nevertheless, the midpoint of the business cycle often marks the turning point for volatility.

Large-Cap U.S. Stocks

Return: Next 3–6 Years = 7–9 percent, Next Ten Years = 9 percent; Volatility: 14–18 percent

As explained in Chapter 1, valuation will not be the driver of stock market returns, as it was during the 1980s and 1990s, when it rose from the single digits into the high-20s. The remainder of this decade is likely to exhibit a relatively narrow price-to-earnings ratio range for the S&P 500 of 14–19 times. This is similar to that of the latter half of the 1960s due to similarities highlighted in Chapter 4. Instead, stock market returns will be driven by earnings growth in the years ahead. Chapter 3 highlighted the fact that, since the 1930s, the long-term secular trend of earnings growth for the large companies in the S&P 500 has been 7 percent. For the remainder of this decade, returns on large-cap U.S. stocks are likely to average within a range of 7–9 percent, based on 7 percent price return (driven by earnings growth) plus a 2 percent dividend yield. This is below the historical total return trend of 12 percent. However, inflation also will remain below the long-term average of 4.5 percent. This means inflation-adjusted returns on stocks may be comparable with the long-term average.

For the remainder of the decade, the volatility of large-cap U.S. stocks will likely be below the 21.7 percent average for 1926–2005 (the full history of the S&P 500 index), given that the economy and financial markets are unlikely to experience challenges similar to the Great Depression or World War II. See Figure 5.1.

Longer economic cycles with fewer boom/bust periods related to inventory cycles have yielded less volatility. Therefore, an analysis of the post-1945 environment serves as a good benchmark timeframe. During the past 60 years, the annual standard deviation for large-cap stock returns averaged 15.8 percent. Importantly, the volatility of large-cap stocks has been fairly consistent over the period. There have been no discernable long-term trends (neither rising nor falling), although

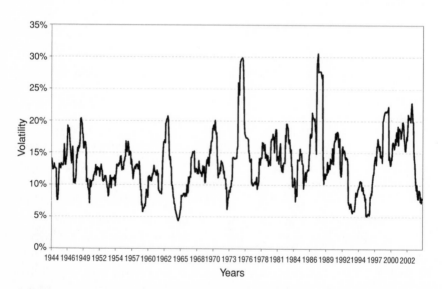

FIGURE 5.1   Volatility of S&P 500 has been stable over time.
Annualized rolling 12 month standard deviation of S&P 500.

there have been spikes, associated with the Arab oil embargo of 1973–74 and the 1987 stock market crash.

This consistency in the trend of volatility exists no matter what year-end timeframe is examined. Traditional measures of standard deviation use a December-to-December 12-month period. Using that measure, volatility for the S&P 500 has averaged 15.8 percent annually over the past 60 years. Interestingly, examining 60 years of data for the other eleven 12-month measurement periods (that is, January-to-January, February-to-February, etc.), the average volatility was somewhat lower, but was within a fairly tight distribution around 15.8 percent—ranging from a low of 14.4 percent for February year-end periods to a high of 17.6 percent for September periods. See Figure 5.2.

The long-term trend in volatility is stable but the pattern of volatility is cyclical. The stock market's volatility cycle is linked to the business cycle. Volatility widens during periods of stress around recessions and narrows as conditions improve during recoveries. This pattern is evident in the chart of the volatility cycle (see Figure 5.3), which illustrates the past 60 years of daily price changes in the S&P 500.

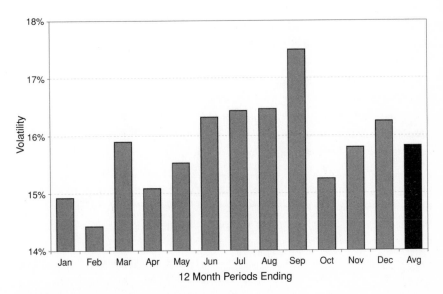

FIGURE 5.2   Stock market volatility by month.
S&P 500 annualized standard deviation for different 12 month periods since 1945.

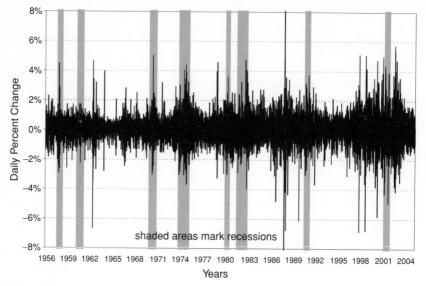

Figure 5.3   Volatility is cyclical.
Daily percent change in S&P 500 since 1955.

There have been only a handful of times when the volatility of the stock market spiked and the economy was not at the end of a business cycle. An extraordinary market shock triggered each occurrence:

- The months leading up to the 1962 Cuban Missile Crisis.
- The stock market crash of October 1987.
- The Asian financial crisis in the fall of 1997.
- The Russian debt default and Fed-organized bailout of the hedge fund Long-Term Capital Management in the fall of 1998.

The federal funds rate has been a good leading indicator of stock market volatility because of its direct link to the current stage of the business cycle. Over the past 40 years, the real fed funds rate (the fed funds rate adjusted for inflation) has typically led stock market volatility by a little over a year, on average. The real federal funds rate bottomed in June of 2004, heralding the return of volatility in 2006.

Because volatility is cyclical, the historical average of past volatility is not always the best predictor of future volatility in any given year. It is important to know the current stage of the cycle in order to assess the likely direction and magnitude of volatility. As I highlight in Chapter 9, this should help in making tactical portfolio adjustments to benefit from volatility.

The recent rapid decline in volatility to cycle-lows is significant. With the exception of the 1988 period, when volatility declined from an abnormally high level related to the stock market crash in 1987, the recent decline is the largest decline in S&P 500 volatility in the past 60 years. Consequently, I expect a cyclical rise in annual volatility in the coming years.

Mid-Capitalization And Small-Capitalization U.S. Stocks

Mid-Cap Return: Next 3–6 Years = 5–7 percent, Next Ten Years = 9 percent; Volatility: 15–20 percent

Small-Cap Return: Next 3–6 Years = 4–6 percent, Next Ten Years = 9 percent; Volatility: 17–23 percent

Over a full market cycle, total returns for large-, mid-, and small-cap stocks are likely to be around 9 percent. However, over the remaining years of this business cycle, I expect mid- and small-cap stocks to underperform large-cap stocks, consistent with the cyclical pattern of relative performance.

For the purpose of this analysis, I am using the Russell 2000 small-cap index to represent small-capitalization stocks because it extends back to 1979. The S&P 600 small-cap index was not introduced until 1994.

Historically, small- and large-cap stocks have offered investors equivalent performance. In fact, since their inception in 1979, the large-cap Russell 1000 and small-cap Russell 2000 have provided average annual total returns that differ by only a few tenths of a percentage point.

As I have often pointed out, earnings have proven to be the most important driver of stock market performance. Earnings have a tighter long-term relationship with stock prices than anything else. While varying slightly from large-cap earnings in any given year, the earnings of small-cap companies have provided the same average pace of growth as large-cap companies (see Figure 5.4). I expect this long-term trend to continue, resulting in similar performance among companies of varying sizes over a full ten-year business cycle.

Despite their similarities when looking at average returns over a long period, stocks of different-sized companies follow different patterns of performance during the course of the business cycle. When returns do not move in tandem, investing among asset categories can produce diversification benefits and opportunities for tactical risk management.

Early in a market cycle, small-cap stocks have typically outperformed large-caps by a wide margin. Investors generally embrace higher-risk small-cap stocks as the economy emerges from recession, as it did in November 1982, March 1991, and November 2001. After the early stages of a market cycle ends, mid- and small-cap stocks have tended to underperform (see Figure 5.5).

In fact, there was only one notable period of small-cap outperformance that was not accompanied by a change in the market cycle. This

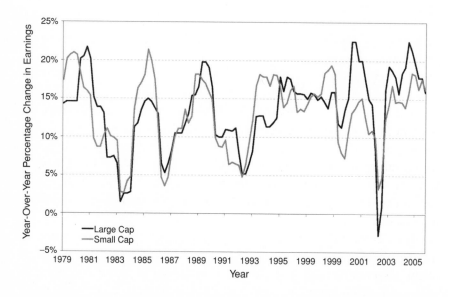

FIGURE 5.4   Large- and small-cap stocks have provided similar earnings growth.
Russell 1000 and Russell 2000 year-over-year earnings growth.

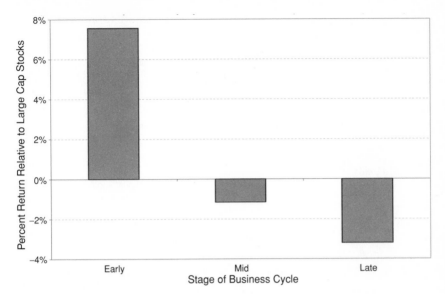

FIGURE 5.5   Small-cap stock relative performance during different stages of the business cycle.
Average performance of small-cap stocks less large-cap stocks over 12 business cycles from 1927–2001 (ex- 4/75–1/80).

period was marked by two regulatory changes: the passage of the Employee Retirement Income Security Act (ERISA) in 1974, which governs the investment activities of pension plans, and the clarification of the "prudent man" rule by the Department of Labor in 1978, which permitted pension plans to own small-cap stocks and other risky investments provided that they did not elevate the risk of the entire portfolio. As a result, pension plans realigned their portfolio allocations consistent with the change in regulation and assets flooded into small- and mid-cap stocks. This caused an unusual late-cycle period of outperformance for small-cap stocks.

The current business cycle has reached the middle stage suggesting the early-cycle period of outperformance by small- and mid-cap stocks likely has ended, leaving these asset classes to underperform for the remainder of the cycle by an average margin of about 2–3 percent. It is worth noting that small-cap total returns offer a different composition than large-caps, owing to their slightly lower dividend yield.

The cyclical pattern of volatility for mid- and small-cap stocks is the same as for large-cap stocks. However, mid-cap stocks tend to exhibit about ten percent more volatility than large-cap stocks on average over a full cycle. Small-caps tend to be 25 percent more volatile than large-caps (see Figure 5.6). The pattern of the volatility of small- and mid-cap stocks relative to large-caps rises through the middle stages of the cycle, when mid-caps and small-caps typically underperform.

International Stocks

Return: Next 3–6 Years = 8–10 percent, Next Ten Years = 10 percent; Volatility: 14–18 percent

Over the long term, international markets are likely to provide return opportunities similar to those of U.S. markets. In the short term, international stocks may outperform U.S. stocks largely because of the impact of an expected decline in the dollar.

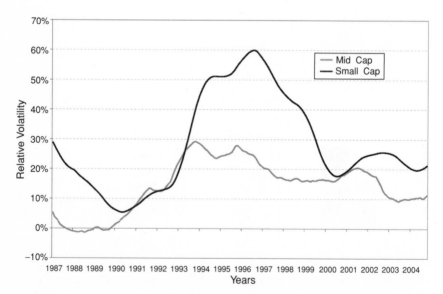

FIGURE 5.6   Volatility of small- and mid-cap stocks relative to large-cap stocks. Three year average of relative 12 month volatility of S&P 400 Mid-Cap and S&P 600 Small-Cap to S&P 500 Large-Cap Index.

International stocks outperformed the S&P 500 during the 1970s and 1980s, but underperformed in the 1990s (see Figure 5.7). There are four primary reasons for this:

- In the 1970s and 1980s, large European nations narrowed their labor productivity gap with the United States. This changed in the 1990s, however, when U.S. productivity growth pushed ahead and growth in Europe slowed. By the end of the 1990s, the labor productivity gap with the United States had widened again. This was related to both the differential in productivity-enhancing information technology investment, as well as regulation that distorted the competitive environment and stifled innovation in Europe.
- The dollar uncharacteristically appreciated in the 1990s. Gains from foreign investment are muted when the investment returns in international markets are translated into a rising dollar.
- Technology stocks, which make up a much larger portion of the U.S. market than those outside the United States, produced strong performance in the 1990s.

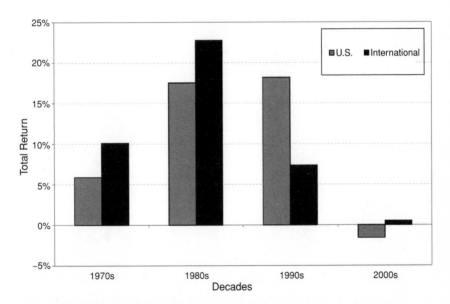

FIGURE 5.7   Annualized performance by decade for U.S. and international stocks. S&P 500 and MSCI EAFE annualized total return by decade.

■ As the 1990s began, the Japanese stock market suffered a tremendous crash (related to the bursting of a real estate bubble) that persisted throughout the decade.

These conditions are unlikely to repeat in the next ten years. In fact,
productivity is rising again overseas. The return on investment is climb-
ing, beginning to close the gap with the United States. Improved prof-
itability is resulting from the pro-business reforms put in place in
Europe and Asia in recent years. Also, the dollar has resumed the long-
term downtrend so far this decade, having fallen 25 percent from its
peak in 2002, boosting international stock performance when translated
back into dollars (gains denominated in international currencies are
worth more in dollar terms when the dollar falls in value).

Historically, international stocks have exhibited volatility very similar
to that of U.S. stocks with the exception of much of the 1990s (see Figure 5.8). Volatility rose for international stocks in the 1990s as international stocks underperformed. I do not expect a repeat of the factors that
led to the deviation in relative volatility in the mid-1990s. My expectation
for international stock volatility is similar to that of the U.S. stock market.

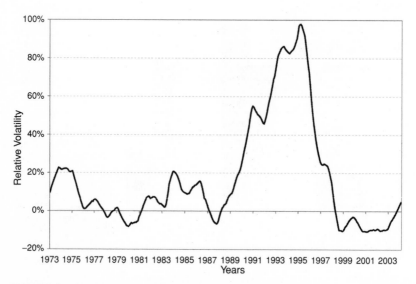

FIGURE 5.8   Volatility of international stocks relative to U.S.
Three year average of 12 month rolling relative standard deviation of MSCI EAFE to
S&P 500.

Taxable Core Bonds

Return: Next 3–6 Years = 4–6 percent, Next Ten Years = 5 percent; Volatility: 4–6 percent

The "core" category of the bond market is the broadest, representing the total of all taxable investment grade bonds (those rated BBB or higher by Standard and Poor's or Baa by Moody's Investors Service). I expect core bond returns, measured by the Lehman Aggregate Bond index, to average 4–6 percent over the remainder of the decade.

Current interest rates are a great predictor of future investment performance. The yield on the intermediate-term government bond index has proven to accurately forecast the performance of that index over the next ten years—even during volatile periods for interest rates. Given the current level of interest rates, the total return on the bond market over the next ten years is likely to be in the mid-single digits (see Figure 5.9). This marks a big change in performance for bonds. The falling interest rates of the last 25 years have resulted in returns double those likely to be achieved in the next ten years for both bonds and stocks.

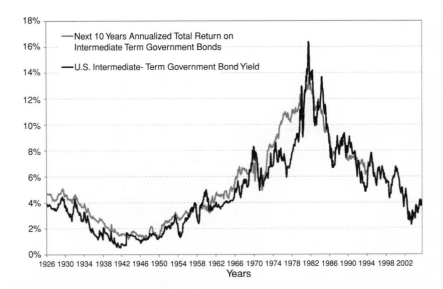

FIGURE 5.9 Yields predict bond returns.
Intermediate term government bond yield and next 10 years annualized total return on intermediate term government bonds.

I have based this outlook for bond market performance on current yields, as well as the impact of shifts in the yield curve and spreads. The currently low level of market interest rates, in conjunction with an outlook for rising interest rates and widening credit spreads, is likely to result in lower-than-average performance across the major sectors of the taxable bond market over the remainder of the decade. See Figure 5.10.

■ Mortgage-Backed Securities—The expected rise in interest rates over the remainder of the decade from multi-decade lows set in 2002 will act to dampen price return in mortgage-backed securities (MBS), the largest component of the investable fixed-income marketplace. In addition, the early 2000s refinancing boom has led to lower coupon rates on MBS, which will further hold down total return on MBS in the years ahead.
■ U.S. Treasury Securities—Treasuries will suffer losses as interest rates rise from near 40-year lows, due to large budget deficits and

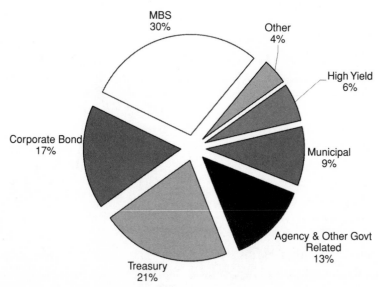

FIGURE 5.10 Total bond market breakdown by sector.
Percentage of market value ($9.7 trillion) as of October 31, 2005.

structural current account imbalances. The historically low coupon rate on Treasury debt will exacerbate these losses. Therefore, I expect mid-single digit returns on Treasuries over the next several years, well below the average of the 1980s and '90s.

- Corporate Bonds—Yield spreads on corporate bonds may remain cyclical. However, having fully recovered after a record widening in 2002, spreads are unlikely to contribute additional capital gains. As with other fixed-income asset classes, the outlook for relatively low (by historical standards) coupon rates and yields will limit income returns from this sector to below the historical averages.
- Agency (Government owned, sponsored, or created entities) Securities—Agencies will continue to be buffeted by regulatory issues and concerns. Given the expected robust issuance of Treasury debt in the remaining years of the decade, it is unlikely that Agency debt will replace Treasuries as the fixed-income market's benchmark of choice (as was once thought). A stable regulatory and governance environment over the rest of the decade, along with a stream of regular and predictable issuance, would enable Agency debt to continue to provide market-like returns (with slightly less volatility than the market as a whole) as the decade progresses.

The historical volatility of the taxable bond market, as measured by annual standard deviation, is 7 percent. This number reflects the high inflation of the late 1970s and early 1980s. I forecast average taxable bond market volatility over the remaining years of this business cycle to be between 4 percent and 6 percent. Embedded within this forecast of volatility is the Fed's effectiveness in managing inflation, economic considerations—such as excess global capital and labor capacity, and the evolving structure and composition of the bond market.

Like stocks, bond market volatility also is linked to the business cycle because economic conditions affect changes in credit spreads. As the economy weakens, credit spreads widen to reflect the rising risk of default, and volatility increases. Bond market volatility and the business cycle are also linked because of inflation. During the past 20 years, the month-to-month changes in consumer prices have exhibited twice the volatility around recessions than during expansions, and this has contributed to overall bond market volatility.

Short-Term Bonds

Return: Next 3–6 Years = 3–5 percent, Next Ten Years = 4 percent; Volatility: 1–3 percent

I expect returns to average 3–5 percent for short-term bonds. The market is currently pricing these defensive bonds to yield the midpoint of the range, or approximately 4 percent. Short-term bonds fare best relative to bonds of longer maturity when interest rates are rising.

Over the next few years, I expect short-term bond volatility to be in line with levels of the past 20 years (after the period of high and volatile inflation in the 1970s and early 1980s).

Long-Term Bonds

Return: Next 3–6 Years = 4–6 percent, Next Ten Years = 5 percent; Volatility: 7–11 percent

I expect a rise in interest rates to moderate the returns on long-term bonds, currently priced to yield around 5 percent.

Long-term bonds have more exposure to interest-rate risk than shorter-term fixed-income securities, causing long-term bonds to have substantially more price volatility (see Figure 5.11). Long-term bond volatility follows a cyclical pattern that rises around transitions in the business cycle. I expect volatility to rise from cycle lows to post an average in line with that of the past 20 years.

High Yield Bonds

Return: Next 3–6 Years = 4–6 percent, Next Ten Years = 6 percent; Volatility: 7–11 percent

High yield bonds (sometimes called junk bonds) generally have a higher risk of default and offer higher yields to compensate for this risk. I expect high-yield bonds to return an average of 4–6 percent for the remainder of the decade, despite their current 7.1 percent yield. This is primarily because default rates are very cyclical and are likely to rise in the coming years. My forecast for high-yield bonds includes the following assumptions, on average:

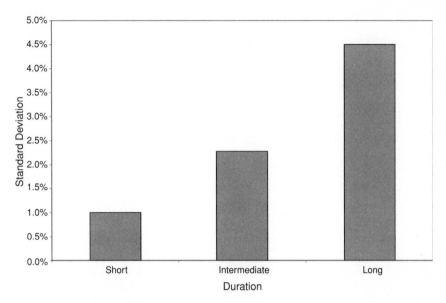

FIGURE 5.11 Bond volatility rises with duration.
Standard deviation of 52 week rolling return of short-, intermediate- and long-term bond indexes over past nine years.

- A 300-basis-point credit spread over Treasuries.
- A default rate of around 3 percent.
- A recovery rate of 35 percent.

I expect that the high-yield default rate has reached its low for this business cycle. I project a 3 percent rate for the remainder of this business cycle. I also expect a recovery rate (recouping principal, interest, or both after a default) of 35 percent, a bit below the historical average, because the high-yield market currently has a greater concentration of CCC-rated debt, which typically experiences a very low recovery rate. I expect defaults to reduce high-yield returns by an average of two percentage points.

The volatility of high-yield bonds is very cyclical. Volatility is at the low end of its range now, and I expect it to increase as the end of the business cycle approaches. In addition, the volatility of the high-yield market has shifted structurally higher from one-half to one standard deviation since the fall of 1998, in the aftermath of the Russian government's default on its bonds because dealers drastically cut their inventory. See Figure 5.12.

International Bonds

Return: Next 3–6 Years = 6–8 percent, Next Ten Years = 5 percent; Volatility: 8–11 percent

Over the long-term, international bonds will likely provide an identical return to high-quality U.S. bonds, but with higher volatility due to currency shifts. The driver of nearly all of the return on unhedged international bonds is the change in the value of the dollar. A falling dollar causes the value of the income stream from the foreign-currency-denominated bonds to be worth more in dollar terms, thereby augmenting total return. Only during periods when the dollar fell materially (as it did in 2002–04, as well as in 1986–87) did unhedged international bonds provide superior performance to U.S. bonds.

I expect returns on international bonds to outperform U.S. bonds, averaging 6–8 percent for the remainder of the decade, as the value of the dollar declines. In addition, European government bond markets should significantly outperform U.S. Treasuries as a combination of

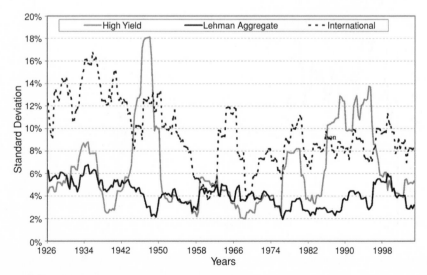

FIGURE 5.12   Bond asset class volatility.
Annualized monthly standard deviation of fixed income benchmarks.

slower economic growth and currency strength (accompanied by some deceleration in inflation) keep their interest rates lower than in the United States. Given that foreign debt is primarily government debt, there is little credit risk.

Currency volatility drives most of the volatility of unhedged international bonds. I expect the annual dollar volatility to be in line with the long-term average that has remained consistent despite extended directional trends in the past.

Municipal Bonds

Return: Next 3–6 Years = 3–5 percent, Next Ten Years = 3–5 percent; Volatility: 4–6 percent

Municipal bonds are currently priced to yield 3.7 percent. These bonds tend to be less interest-rate sensitive than their taxable counterparts are and offer yields about 15 percent less than comparable Treasuries because of their tax-advantaged status. I expect municipal bond returns to average 3–5 percent over the remainder of the decade. The volatility of municipal bonds tends to be similar, on average, to that of taxable bonds. See Figure 5.13.

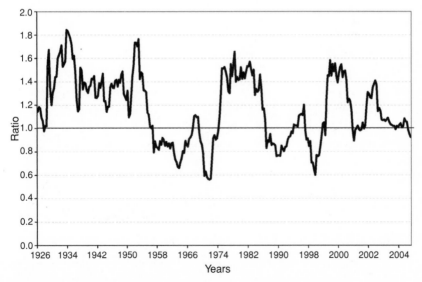

FIGURE 5.13 Municipal bond volatility relative to taxable bond market volatility. Ratio of municipal to core bond 12 month standard deviation.

Cash

Return: Next 3–6 Years = 3 percent, Next Ten Years = 3 percent; Volatility: 1 percent

I expect inflation to remain low (by historical standards) over the remainder of the decade. Therefore, a lower-than-average return on cash, represented by 3-month Treasury Bills, is likely. Our expectation of a muted pace of inflation in the 2000s is based on our forecast for continued productivity growth, intense global competition, and a prescient Fed.

Since 1950, the return on a 3-month T-Bill has outpaced the Consumer Price Index by roughly 100 basis points, although the performance varies widely by decade.

- Over the 1970s, inflation outpaced the return on T-Bills by 100 basis points.
- In the 1980s, inflation was volatile—it started out the decade at a high level, decelerated, and then reaccelerated as the decade ended. During the 1980s, T-bills outperformed inflation by almost 400 basis points.

On balance, I expect the relatively stable and historically benign inflation environment that we have seen over the first part of the decade to persist through the end of the decade. In addition, I believe that the relationship between inflation and the returns on T-Bills that has persisted since 2000 will continue throughout the decade.

This suggests that cash will outpace inflation by roughly 50 basis points, on average, over the rest of the decade, leaving returns on cash at the upper end of our expected 2–3 percent average pace of inflation over the remainder of the decade.

While not static, cash is the least volatile asset class. I expect a standard deviation of around 1 percent.

PART II

The Market-Based Portfolio

In Part I, I described why investors face a challenging environment as the drivers of investment performance undergo an evolutionary change likely to result in financial market performance below the average of recent decades. A new approach to investing that incorporates an adaptive, market-based framework for portfolio construction and heightened degree of tactical adjustment is necessary to manage risk, exploit opportunities, and achieve performance goals in the coming years.

While analyzing historical data and relationships can be useful, forward-looking thinking is very important because relationships can change over time and future returns may differ from those of the past for a variety of reasons. As pointed out in the first part of this book, the past several decades are not a good guide to what the future may hold. As a result, one should not base decisions regarding the investments used to construct a portfolio and their relative weighting within a portfolio purely on market history. Asset returns, risks, and interrelationships have evolved.

A new approach to portfolio construction is required to meet the challenges of the new era of investment performance. The simple yet powerful method—one I refer to as the market-based portfolio—yields a robust asset allocation that is defined relative to many alternative ways the future may evolve, which makes risk estimation more reliable and achieving investment goals more likely. This section details the dynamic and robust investment framework that I propose to meet the challenges of the new market environment.

There are millions of individual securities available to investors. Therefore, it is very important to start with a top-down approach to constructing a portfolio, or asset allocation. Chapter 6 focuses on establishing an investment plan and the most basic investment decision: the allocation between stocks and bonds. Chapter 7 defines which categories of stock and bond investments have the greatest potential to achieve investment goals. Chapter 8 presents the market-based strategic asset allocation framework. The basis and tools for adaptation via tactical asset allocation are provided in Chapter 9. And, Chapter 10 focuses on the data used for tactical asset allocation—what to look for, where to find it, and how to interpret it.

CHAPTER 6

The Investment Plan

This chapter presents the concept of the investment plan and the asset allocations designed to meet a range of goals.

The goal of every investment portfolio is to produce the best outcome over a specific period of time. However, everyone's goals are different. If we all desired the same balance of safety, performance, maintenance, and cost, we would all drive the same type of car. Achieving one's investment goals requires knowing what outcome would define success, assessing whether that objective is realistic in today's new era of investment performance, and constructing an asset allocation designed to meet that objective.

Therefore, the key to an investment plan is to establish a portfolio, or asset allocation, that contains the most appropriate assets, and the relative weightings of those assets, tailored to achieve realistic performance objectives. The success of an investment plan is heavily dependent on the process used to determine and manage asset allocation.

Well-defined preferences for portfolio risk and return, along with a specified time period, provide a road map for a well-constructed asset allocation to follow. In addition, establishing an asset allocation tailored to these objectives provides a basis for consistent evaluation of the progress toward achievement of those objectives and for measurement of the success of the investment plan.

Realistic goals are important to a successful investment plan. In Part I, I described the outlook for financial market performance during the next 10 years. Not even the most aggressive investor should expect returns at or above the long-term stock market's average annualized performance of 12 percent.

It is important to note that, in developing an investment plan, the goal is not to attempt to beat the market. The investment universe offers many more opportunities than just the large-capitalization U.S. stocks represented by the major market indexes. An investor who is focused solely on attempting to meet or beat a particular index with his or her portfolio is better suited to asset-class-specific investing, rather than asset allocation, which is capable of delivering a far broader range of performance objectives. In other words, a portfolio comprised only of large-cap U.S. stocks is more likely to come close to meeting or beating the S&P 500 on a regular basis than a portfolio diversified among many types of assets. However, the variability of investment performance is likely to be much higher for a stock-only portfolio compared with the asset allocated portfolio.

Despite the fact that individual assets are often volatile, different types of assets can be combined to effectively manage risk, enhancing the predictability of portfolio returns. For example, a 65 percent stock and 35 percent bond asset allocation has, on average, delivered around 90 percent of the total return of the S&P 500 by capturing 80 percent of the upside of the stock market while only suffering 40 percent of the downside, measured over rolling 12 month periods of time since 1960.

Rather than simply concentrating on beating a stock market index, the market-based strategic asset allocation framework presented in the next few chapters will provide a carefully constructed vehicle (as different as a Volvo and a Ferrari—yet equally effective) to achieve a unique performance objective. As a result, the success of the investment plan must be measured as progress toward the stated investment objective, rather than by a single market index.

An investment plan:

- Involves a strategic asset allocation tailored to achieving specific objectives.
- Establishes a road map to unique long-term objectives.
- Allows for a consistent basis for evaluation of progress in achieving those objectives.
- Moves beyond thinking only of S&P 500 performance as an appropriate benchmark.

Six Strategic Asset Allocations

I have provided six asset allocations of traditional assets to use as guides (see Table 6.1). The six asset allocations provide a full spectrum of long-term risk and return objectives. The primary difference in return and risk is determined by the mix between stocks, bonds, and cash-equivalent investments (since the stock asset class allocations are proportional for the most part), with stocks having historically offered both higher returns and risk relative to bonds and cash, and cash having offered the lowest return and least risk.

Since 1926, 26 percent of stock market and 8 percent of bond market returns were negative on a 12-month basis. However, only rarely—about 1 percent of the time—did both stocks and bonds post simultaneous year-over-year negative returns. Therefore, managing the stock/bond allocation can have a significant impact on the stability and predictability of portfolio performance. This also shows that incorporating cash equivalents, very short-term interest paying investments, into a strategic asset allocation is appropriate for only the most conservative of investors, since 99 percent of the time stocks or bonds have provided better performance.

Proper asset allocation greatly increases the likelihood that portfolios will offer returns with greater stability, and therefore, predictability. Each of the six asset allocations presented differs from the next in the stock/bond/cash weighting by about 15–20 percent. These increments are just enough to result in materially different risk and return characteristics for the asset allocations. They leave no gaps or redundancies in the risk and return spectrum. The impact of these increments is to vary the return and risk characteristics of the strategic asset allocations by a little more than 0.5 percent in potential return (0.6–0.8 percent) and about 3–5 percent in potential 12-month downside. Offering additional asset allocation profiles with even more refined graduations in stock/bond allocations with return or risk expectations that would vary by 0.25 percent in annual return, and 2 percent in potential loss, would imply a false sense of precision for what is a volatile and dynamic relationship among asset classes.

The stock and bond allocation is very powerful at controlling risk, but only to a degree, given the volatility of returns and the relationship between stocks and bonds. Historically, stocks have rarely provided their average 12 percent annualized return and have varied, on aver-

TABLE 6.1 Six Strategic Asset Allocations

	Preservation	Conservative	Moderate	Balanced	Growth	Aggressive
Traditional Asset Allocation						
U.S. Stocks						
Large Cap Growth	7.5%	12.0%	17.0%	22.5%	27.5%	34.5%
Large Cap Value	7.5%	12.0%	17.0%	22.5%	27.5%	34.5%
Mid Cap Growth		2.0%	2.0%	2.5%	3.5%	4.0%
Midl Cap Value		2.0%	2.0%	2.5%	3.5%	4.0%
Small Cap Growth			1.0%	1.0%	1.0%	1.5%
Small Cap Value			1.0%	1.0%	1.0%	1.5%
Total U.S. Stocks	15.0%	28.0%	40.0%	52.0%	64.0%	80.0%
International Stocks						
Large Cap Growth		3.5%	5.0%	6.0%	7.5%.	9.5%
Large Cap Value		3.5%	5.0%	6.0%	7.5%	9.5%
Small Cap				1.0%	1.0%	1.0%
Total International Stocks		7.0%	10.0%	13.0%	16.0%	20.0%
Total Equity	15.0%	35.0%	50.0%	65.0%	80.0%	100.0%
U.S. Core Bonds*	30.0%	65.0%	50.0%	35.0%	20.0%	
Cash	55.0%					
Total Traditonal Allocation	100.0%	100.0%	100.0%	100.0%	100.0%	100.0%
Allocation with Alternative Investments**						
Stocks	15.0%	30.0%	42.0%	50.0%	58.0%	70.0%
Bonds	25.0%	60.0%	43.0%	30.0%	17.0%	
Cash	55.0%					
Alternative	5.0%	10.0%	15.0%	20.0%	25.0%	30.0%
Total with Alternatives	100.0%	100.0%	100.0%	100.0%	100.0%	100.0%

*Tactical bond asset classes such as high yield or international bonds have no strategic weighting
**The allocation to Alternative Assets is discussed in Chapter 10.

age, by 8 percentage points from one year to the next. While bonds have tended to moderate volatility by moving in the opposite direction of stocks, the relationship hasn't always been constant. In fact, as I highlighted in Chapter 1, stocks and bonds have had a dynamic relationship over time—sometimes moving in opposite directions for a long period of time (providing effective risk diversification), then in the same direction for a long period, and then back again. This can be seen in Figure 1.8. I expect the next 10 years to result in an environment where stocks and bonds tend to move more in opposite directions than the historical average, providing a higher degree of diversification than in the past.

It is easy to see the impact on a portfolio of the stock/bond allocation by looking back at historical performance. Positive year-over-year returns have been delivered on rolling 12 month returns since 1950 ranging from 99 percent of the time for the blend of assets labeled Preservation (15 percent Stocks/30 percent Bonds/55 percent cash equivalents) asset allocation, to 80 percent of the time for the blend of assets in the Growth (80/20/0) asset allocation.

Balanced Asset Allocation is 65 percent Equity and 35 percent Fixed Income

Some may find it odd to label the 65/35 allocation as balanced, when 50/50 demonstrates an obvious balance between stock and bond investments. However, for a long-term investor it is a balance of risk and return, not of stocks and bonds, that is most important; I believe that balance is best achieved by a 65/35 allocation.

This can be illustrated by the fact that a 65/35 mix is the highest allocation to stocks that has never had a rolling five-year period with a loss since 1946 (post-World War II) using monthly data. Since I view a five-year period as the minimum period that would constitute a long-term investment holding period, we consider the 65/35 allocation to be generally the best balance of risk and return for a long-term investor.

In addition, the balanced allocation has the potential for a most likely lowest return of around 13 percent in any one-year period; a level of risk that I believe is reasonable for the average long-term investor. See Figure 6.1.

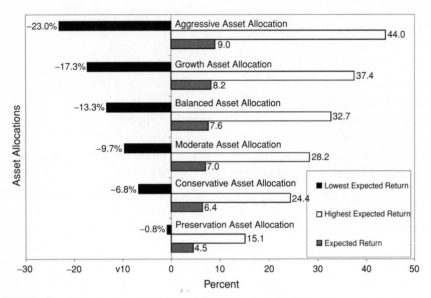

FIGURE 6.1   Expected range of returns by strategic asset allocation.

CHAPTER 7

Asset Classes

With the millions of individual securities available to an investor, it is very important to start with a top-down approach to constructing a portfolio, or asset allocation. The first step in designing an asset allocation is to determine which broad categories of investments have the greatest potential to achieve a wide range of risk and return objectives. This chapter presents the asset classes that constitute the strategic asset allocation.

Asset Class Criteria

An asset class is a group of investments with similar characteristics. It is helpful to group similar types of investments together into asset classes in order to better forecast their contribution to the performance of a diversified portfolio. Why? Because the performance of an individual security is difficult to predict with accuracy. This is as true as it has ever been. In fact, over the past 40 years the variability of the returns of individual securities has increased steadily. It is therefore essential to diversify *within* an asset class in order to reduce volatility and increase the likelihood of achieving a targeted rate of return over the long term.

When constructing a diversified portfolio to satisfy a long-term investment objective, appropriate asset classes should possess:

■ Investability—the asset class must consist of securities available to a U.S.-based investor and offer sufficient liquidity to allow for efficient buying and selling.

■ Long history—the asset class must have a track record over at least two business cycles, so that performance behavior can be analyzed and consistency of characteristics can be assessed.

■ Well-defined—the characteristics and performance behavior of the securities within an asset class should be similar to each other, but should differ from securities in different asset classes in order to obtain the benefits of risk diversification.

I include asset classes that, when combined in a broadly diversified allocation, contribute meaningfully to the expected return and/or risk reduction of the entire mix of assets. In other words, a group of securities qualifies for use as an asset class in a recommended asset allocation if it, as a class, contributes something to an otherwise well-diversified portfolio. If the group of securities does not contribute much to either risk reduction or portfolio return, then it is not worth including as a strategic asset class in a portfolio.

What Groups of Investments Are Not Strategic Asset Classes?

To qualify as an asset class, the behavior and performance of the individual investments within the group should be similar. In other words, the correlations among the investments in the group should be relatively high. An example of a group of investments that does *not* constitute an asset class is commodities, because they act remarkably dissimilar to each other. The performance of most categories of commodities departs dramatically from the average. The typical correlation of individual commodities with the overall group average is near zero. For example, the biggest commodity category is energy; it has demonstrated an inverse relationship to changes in the prices of other major commodity categories like industrials, precious metals, livestock, and agricultural products. As a group, commodities have tended to track inflation and have provided returns in line with inflation over the long term, but have done so with a lot of volatility. Commodities do not meet the definition of an asset class.

An example of a group of investments that *does* constitute an asset class, but does not qualify for inclusion in a strategic, long-term asset allocation, is international bonds. The international bond asset class is likely to provide an identical return to high-quality U.S. bonds, but with higher risk because of currency shifts. Only during 1986–87 and 2003–04, when the U.S. dollar collapsed, did unhedged international bonds provide superior performance (outpacing U.S. bonds by an average of 19 percentage points). The dollar may depreciate from time to time, but I do not expect a sharp and linear decline in the dollar over the long term. As a result, international bonds are not an appropriate strategic or long-term (defined as a full ten-year economic cycle) asset class for a diversified portfolio. Nevertheless, it may make sense occasionally to allocate assets to unhedged international bonds on a tactical basis, depending on the outlook for the dollar.

There are three traditional asset classes I will focus on here: cash-equivalent investments (commonly referred to as cash), fixed income (bonds), and equity (stocks). I will address alternative or non-traditional investments (such as hedge funds) separately in Chapter 10.

Equity Asset Classes

Equity markets are broken down into asset classes based on a stock's style classification, as well as the issuing company's size and the geographic location of its main base of operations. The nine equity asset classes as defined by style, size, and geography are: U.S. Large-Cap Growth, U.S. Large-Cap Value, U.S. Mid-Cap Growth, U.S. Mid-Cap Value, U.S. Small-Cap Growth, U.S. Small-Cap Value, International Growth, International Value, and International Small-Cap.

Style

The importance of style as an investment classification became clear at the start of the 1970s, with the phenomenon known as the "Nifty 50" (see Table 7.1). An elite group of 50 fast-growing companies, with household names like Xerox Corporation and Polaroid Corporation, began to dominate the stock market like no group before. For a period

TABLE 7.1   Nifty Fifty 1972

American Express	First National City	PepsiCo
American Home Products	General Electric	Pfizer
American Hospital Supply	Gillette	Phillip Morris
AMP	Halliburton	Polaroid
Anheuser-Busch	Heublein	Procter & Gamble
Avon Products	IBM	Revlon
Baxter Travenol	Intl Flavors & Fragrances	Schering
Black & Decker	ITT	Schlitz Brewing
Bristol-Myers	J.C. Penney	Schlumberger
Burroughs	Johnson & Johnson	Sears Roebuck
Chesebrough Ponds	Kresge	Simplicity Pattern
Coca-Cola	Louisiana Land & Exploration	Squibb
Digital Equipment	Lubrizon	Texas Instruments
Dow Chemical	McDonald's	Upjohn
Eastman Kodak	Merck	Walt Disney
Eli Lilly	MGIC Investment	Xerox
Emery Air Freight	Minnesota Mining	

of four years, the performance of these rapidly growing companies strongly outpaced the rest of the market. Then, at the start of the great bear market of 1973–74, investors pulled back from these high-flying stocks more than most others and set off a multi-year period in which more reasonably valued stocks were favored by investors. This marked the first of many style cycles in which growth stocks and value stocks oscillated in a mirror image of each other around the market trend.

Over the long term, growth stocks and value stocks offer similar performance. However, for periods of a few years, one style tends to be in favor, outperforming the out-of-favor style by an average of 8 percent on an annualized basis. Then, roles reverse and the previously out-of-favor style outperforms.

There are many ways of defining style (see Table 7.2). In fact, there is no universal agreement about how precisely to define specific styles. It is generally agreed, however, that there are significant differences in the performance characteristics of growth and value stocks. Thus, style is a useful means of classifying asset classes.

TABLE 7.2 Comparison of Various Firms' Style Classification Criteria

	Growth	Value	Reconstituted
S&P*	• Higher 5-year EPS growth rate • Higher 5-year sales per share growth rate • Higher 5-year internal growth rate (Net Income × Asset Turnover × Leverage × Retention Ratio)	• Lower Price-to-Book ratio • Lower Cash flow-to-Price ratio • Lower Sales-to-Price ratio • Higher dividend yield	Annually on 12/31
Russell*	• Higher Price-to-Book ratio • HIgher forecasted earnings growth rate	• Lower Price-to-Book ratio • Lower forecasted earnings growth rate	Annually on 6/30
MSCI*	• Higher long-term and short-term forward EPS growth rate • Higher current internal growth rate • Higher long-term EPS growth trend • Higher long-term sales per share growth trend	• Lower Price-to-Book ratio • Lower forward Price-to-Earnings ratio • Higher dividend yield	Semi-Annually
Ibbotson	• Higher Price-to-Earnings ratio • Higher Price-to-Book ratio • Pays little or no dividend • High growth of earnings and sales	• Lower Price-to-Earnings ratio • Lower Price-to-Book ratio • Higher dividend yields • Slower growth of earnings and sales	Annually
Lipper	• Above average Price-to-Book ratio • Above average Price-to-Earnings ratio • Above average 3-year historical sales-per-share growth	• Below average Price-to-Book ratio • Below average Price-to-Earnings ratio • Below average 3-year historical sales-per-share growth	Monthly
Morningstar	• Higher Price-to-Earnings and Price-to-Book ratios relative to other companies of similar size in the same industry	• Lower Price-to-Earnings and Price-to-Book ratios relative to other companies of similar size in the same industry	Quarterly

* Stocks can be classified partially as growth and partially as value.

Value stocks tend to offer lower relative valuations and slower rates of earnings growth than growth stocks. Why allocate to both growth and value styles? The performance of the two styles is complementary—they balance each other while oscillating around the overall market trend.

Size

Size is a key factor in defining asset classes. Companies of different sizes face different challenges with regard to end-markets, access to capital, business concentration (smaller firms tend to produce just a few products, or sell to just one or two big customers), management depth (smaller firms are more likely to have just a few key decision-makers who would be difficult to replace), and liquidity.

Size is commonly defined by a stock's market capitalization, which falls into three asset categories:

- Large—stocks with a market capitalization above $4 billion.
- Mid—stocks with a market capitalization between $1 billion and $4 billion.
- Small—stocks with a market capitalization between $250 million and $1 billion.

Stocks with capitalizations below $250 million are called "micro-cap." The stock of companies with very small market capitalizations generally are not considered an asset class because the characteristics and performance behavior of the stocks are not similar. In my view, stocks that are of micro-cap size demonstrate idiosyncrasies in performance and do not behave in a similar enough fashion to be considered part of one cohesive asset class, and can not be treated as a traditional asset class.

Large-cap stocks dominate the market. This asset class comprises about 85 percent of the total investable U.S. stock market of companies with market values above $250 million. Nevertheless, I do not recommend avoiding the remaining 15 percent of the stock market. A portfolio may benefit from an allocation to small- or mid-cap stocks for a number of reasons.

■ Though they offer similar returns to large-cap stocks, small- and mid-cap stocks offer some risk-diversification benefit. Small- and mid-cap stocks tend to move more independently from large-cap stocks in the early and late stages of the business cycle. Due to the unique nature of the market cycle in early 2000, these benefits were more pronounced. Remarkably, mid- and small-cap stocks, measured by the S&P 400 (mid-cap) and S&P 600 (small-cap) moved very independently of large-cap stocks over the five years ended 2005.

■ Individual investors often overlook smaller companies, many of which are not closely followed by Wall Street analysts. This creates a less efficient marketplace with potentially attractive return opportunities for active investors.

■ Generally, the stocks of smaller companies tend to magnify market performance on the upside and the downside. This creates potential tactical opportunities to manage risk and return.

Geography

Investing a portion of assets in international markets may offer the opportunity to diversify and gain exposure to investment opportunities not found in the United States.

The traditional evidence in support of investing internationally is that international and domestic markets do not always move in the same direction; they exhibit varying degrees of correlation. The thinking goes that combining both international and domestic equities helps to diversify risk by reducing the volatility of their combined performance relative to individual markets. Well, at least this was true in the past. This relationship has not proven valuable in recent years. The correlations between the international and domestic markets have been rising over the past ten years as stock markets around the world have become more integrated and cross-border mergers have flourished. In addition, during periods of global distress when the need to diversify risk is greater, correlations have proven to move higher because all markets are affected negatively. The correlation between the Morgan Stanley Capital International Europe, Australia, and the Far East (MSCI EAFE) Index and the S&P 500 over the past few years has been very high at 0.97.

You Can't Get There From Here

Unfortunately, you can not obtain international exposure simply by owning U.S.-based multinational companies, such as Exxon Mobil Corporation, Merck & Co., Inc., or Citigroup Inc. Based on past stock price behavior, these multinational companies have not demonstrated an ability to provide international diversification benefits.

Actually, the stocks of U.S.-based multinational companies behave more like U.S. stocks than the geographic breakdown of their revenues may imply. One reason is that these stocks are big components of the major U.S. stock market indexes. They tend to be owned largely by U.S. investors who buy them to get U.S. market exposure; thus, their buying and selling typically reflects the economic and market outlook for the United States. Another reason is that the stocks of U.S.-based multinational companies do not offer the same degree of exposure to non-U.S. tax regimes, political risks, regulations, and legal systems as non-U.S.-based companies.

The factors that drive their performance tend to be global industry dynamics, such as commodity prices (as is the case for large companies in the energy sector), or their home-market conditions, such as changes in regulation (in the case of the pharmaceutical industry and the financial sector).

Alternatively, not all multinational companies are based in the United States. Many are very large international companies. In fact, measured by market capitalization, seven non-U.S. companies rank among the world's top ten in the energy sector, six in materials and telecommunication services sectors, five in utilities, and four in the financials, consumer staples, and consumer discretionary sectors. Investors would miss the opportunities to own many of the world's leading companies without an allocation to international stocks.

The correlation between U.S. and international equities is unlikely to drop back to the lows of decades ago, given the higher degree of global integration and the rise of multinational corporations. Nevertheless, correlations above 0.90 are unlikely to continue. Therefore, some diversification benefit is likely to return. The prior periods of relatively

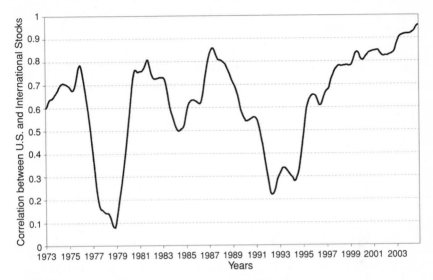

FIGURE 7.1 Correlation of U.S. and international stocks.
Three year average correlation of S&P 500 and MSCI EAFE indexes on 12 month rolling basis.

high global stock market correlation took place during periods of stress (see Figure 7.1):

- From late 1973 through 1976, the Arab oil embargo caused correlations to surge and remain at high levels; however, in 1977, correlations fell sharply.
- The global recession that took place in the early 1980s drove correlations higher.
- The months surrounding the 1987 stock market crash resulted in elevated correlations.
- The current period of high correlation began soon after the Russian debt default in 1998.

Beyond the benefits of diversification and exposure to many of the world's leading companies, there are other potential benefits to investing outside the U.S., including the unique opportunities associated with Asia and Europe. International companies offer deeper penetration into faster growing markets. A growing workforce and rising middle class in many parts of Asia, such as China, offer a potentially powerful new source of demand for goods and services that may disproportionately benefit local and regional providers.

Investors should expect international markets to provide returns similar to those of the U.S. market. International stocks have performed in line with or outperformed the S&P 500 during the 1960s, 1970s, and 1980s, but underperformed in the 1990s. There are three primary reasons for the underperformance in the 1990s.

- The dollar appreciated. When investors convert their foreign-currency denominated gains into U.S. dollars, their investment return is reduced by a rise in the dollar.
- Technology stocks, which make up a much larger portion of the U.S. market than those outside the United States, exhibited strong performance.
- The Japanese stock market suffered a tremendous crash as the 1990s began, with persistent weakness throughout the decade related to the bursting of a real estate asset bubble.

To assume that U.S. stocks will offer a repeat of the 1990s investment performance and an indefinitely higher return than international stocks, one would have to believe that:

- The value of the dollar will steadily rise against the currencies of U.S. trading partners.
- There will be powerful multi-year outperformance by technology stocks.
- An overseas asset bubble will burst, even though asset price imbalances are not near extremes.
- The United States is a riskier place to invest and investors require a higher return to compensate for the additional risk.

These required assumptions are counterintuitive and hard to defend. Some may argue that the U.S. economy is more efficient and more flexible than its foreign counterparts. Unfortunately, this gap is closing and not widening. It would have to widen to sustain U.S. stock market outperformance. It is more reasonable to assume that the United States and other developed markets will have similar long-term expected returns.

Fixed-Income Asset Classes

Fixed-income performance is primarily determined by credit quality and changes in interest rates (measured commonly by duration, which I'll explain shortly) rather than by sector or issuer type. This is similar to classifying the U.S. equity market by size and style rather than sector or industry.

Defining asset classes by duration and quality, rather than as a particular sector of the fixed-income marketplace (such as government bonds or corporate bonds) makes sense because both duration and quality vary widely within each of these traditional fixed-income sectors. Allocating only by issuer type, without regard to duration and quality, can lead to making unintended bets on quality and duration, which are more influential factors affecting performance.

As noted earlier, a key definition of an asset class is that it has low correlations with other asset classes, but a high correlation among the investments within the asset class. Over the past 15 years, the correlation among the major sectors (corporate bonds, government bonds, mortgage-backed securities, agency bonds, asset-backed securities, and Treasuries) was quite high (at least 0.85–0.90). However, the correlation across the range of credit quality and duration was much lower, yielding effective diversification potential for an asset allocation.

Credit Quality

The correlation over the past 15 years between high-yield (low-quality) and investment-grade (high-quality) corporate debt was quite low, around 0.35. The correlation between high-yield bonds and the overall fixed-income universe was even lower, at 0.22. Thus, managing the asset allocation with regard to credit quality can add significant diversification to the fixed-income portion of the allocation.

The low correlation across the range of fixed-income credit quality implies that bonds with high credit ratings perform materially differently from those with low credit ratings. They do, and this has to do with the business cycle.

■ Lower-quality bonds perform well when the economy is accelerating, improving the ability of companies to service their debt. They also fare better when interest rates are rising, given their higher yields.

■ Higher-quality bonds tend to perform best when the economy is weakening and the safety of higher-quality companies is preferred to the relatively higher risk of bankruptcy associated with lower-quality companies. The generally lower yields provide more interest-rate sensitivity.

Duration

The single most important factor affecting the performance of fixed-income assets is interest rates. Duration measures the sensitivity of a fixed-income instrument to changes in interest rates. It factors how much life is remaining on a bond, as well as the size of its interest or coupon payment. (The longer the time to maturity on a bond, all else being equal, the higher its duration. The lower the interest payment on a bond, all else being equal, the higher its duration.)

Longer-duration securities are more sensitive to changes in rates. As rates rise, the value of a bond typically falls and, conversely, as rates fall the value of a bond rises. The impact can be dramatic. For example, a 1 percent rise in long-term interest rates would reduce the value of a 30-year government bond by about 15 percent, while the same change in short-term rates would shave only 2 percent off of a 2-year note.

As is the case with credit quality, defining asset class by duration adds more value to an overall asset allocation than allocating by issuer type. The correlation between the return on the 2-year Treasury Note and the 30-year Treasury Bond is well under 0.80, suggesting that duration constitutes an asset class more appropriately than issuer type.

CHAPTER 8

Strategic Asset Allocation

The strategic asset allocation is the long-term baseline weighting of the asset classes. This chapter will present the market-based framework for the construction of a robust strategic asset allocation.

The goal of any investment plan is to establish, as accurately as possible, a combination of assets that will produce the desired portfolio objectives over a specified time period. While analyzing historical data and detailed financial models is useful, forward-looking thinking also is very important, because relationships can change over time and future returns may differ from past returns for a variety of reasons. Investors should not establish baseline asset class weightings based purely on market history. The past is not a perfect guide to what will unfold in the future.

Asset class returns, risks, and inter-relationships may structurally shift over time.

■ For the past 20 years, total returns for bonds have been boosted by falling interest rates—a trend that is unlikely to continue. Total returns on bonds may lag long-term historical averages.

■ The structure of the universe of growth stocks has changed over time. It was once a relatively defensive group of stocks dominated by the health care and consumer staples sectors. Now, with the technology sector a much larger portion of the growth stock universe, its volatility has increased. The volatility of growth stocks may exceed the long-term historical average.

■ The relationship, or correlation, between asset classes may differ from prior periods. For example, the correlation between stocks and bonds has changed over time. It has recently become negative, meaning that stock prices and bond prices move inversely to each other. Of the potential range of +1 to −1 the relationship has ranged from +0.6 to −0.6 during the past 75 years.

The best way to manage risk—in investing or any other dynamic discipline—is through analysis and modeling. Extensive quantitative analysis of historical data and complex modeling of possible future outcomes form the basis of sound decision-making. However, the process cannot stop there. Because financial markets are ever changing, it is critical that the output of analytical models be fine-tuned using experience, expertise, and judgment. In short, over-reliance on the raw data produced by a model can be problematic if that which is being measured is evolving and changing. And financial markets are evolving.

This type of approach to managing risk—combining analysis and modeling with experience and judgment—has some impressive followers and practitioners, not the least of which is the Federal Reserve Board. The Fed uses its own variation of tactical risk control to manage the monetary policy of the United States.

> *The Board staff, for example, uses an eclectic approach that includes a number of components, including data analysis, statistical techniques, a suite of econometric models, and judgment.*
>
> —Federal Reserve Chairman Ben S. Bernanke

> *...we policymakers, rather than relying solely on the specific linkages expressed in our formal models, have tended to draw from broader, though less mathematically precise, hypotheses of how the world works.*
>
> —Former Federal Reserve Chairman Alan Greenspan

My method for determining the appropriate weights for stocks and bonds yields a robust asset allocation that is defined relative to many alternative ways the future may evolve, which make returns and risk estimates more reliable.

Mean-Variance Optimization

A common practice to determine the asset class weightings is a quantitative modeling technique called mean-variance optimization. The goal is to create a portfolio with the highest rate of return for a given level of risk. Although the mean-variance approach is used widely by practitioners, it is also widely acknowledged to contain many flaws.

The main shortcoming is that the asset class weights obtained through the mean-variance approach are very sensitive to small changes in the model's inputs. These inputs consist of estimates for return, standard deviation, and correlations for each asset class.

With a single-point estimate for this set of inputs, mean-variance optimizations seeking to maximize expected return or reduce risk often arrive at asset allocations with extreme asset weights. These extreme positions result in outlier asset allocations that depend strongly on a unique set of input assumptions tied to only one potential future course of events. Outliers are, by definition, unstable and unlikely statistical events.

Without recognizing that return estimates are only *estimates* and therefore incorporating a range of possible returns, an optimization will over-concentrate the asset allocation in a few asset classes without the practical consideration of other asset classes that may be insignificantly statistically inferior, yet provide desired stability and diversification.

Using mean-variance optimization, portfolios' allocations often concentrate in just a few asset classes. My method of defining the strategic asset allocation results in a more diversified and, in my view, less risky asset allocation that is more likely to meet investment objectives than a simple mean-variance-optimized allocation

Equity Asset Class Weightings by Style

By definition, half of the stocks in the market are growth stocks and half are value stocks. Remember, there is no material difference in long-term performance. Therefore, strategic asset allocations should be spread evenly across styles, reflecting no long-term bias toward the growth or value style.

The commonly used Russell Growth and Value benchmarks extend back to January of 1979 and demonstrate that there has been no consistent long-term outperformance by either style. Supporting this view, the S&P 500 Growth and Value indexes reflect no consistent trend in relative performance between the style benchmarks from their inception in the mid-1970s. The S&P 500 Growth and Value indexes, from inception until the end of 2005, have each outperformed about half of the time, with value outperforming in 17 of the 30 years.

Historically, every few years one style outperforms the other and then this reverses. Over the long term, I do not believe one style will consistently outperform the other. The equal baseline weighting by style reflects this view, and provides the basis for making tactical bias toward different styles as they are in favor.

Equity Asset Class Weightings by Capitalization

Style is allocated equally because of the similar long-term expected performance for growth and value, and because the market is divided equally among the two. However, simply allocating one-third of U.S. stock market exposure each to large-, mid-, and small-cap stocks does not make sense; market cap is not evenly divided across the three categories. Less than 20 percent of total U.S. market (non-micro) capitalization falls into the mid- and small-cap stock asset classes combined. Allocating equally across capitalizations would suggest that small- and mid-cap stocks are substantially undervalued by the market.

My current baseline asset allocation addresses the weakness of mean-variance optimization and incorporates a number of different potential investment environments. I include a range of forecasts for return, standard deviation, and correlation for each asset class. I have determined the estimate ranges, discussed in Part 1, through careful analysis, models and, yes, judgment. Essentially, I have incorporated the potential variability of outcomes to create an allocation that is more intuitive and more reliable. This transforms the optimization by reducing dependence on historical data, that may not reflect the future, and on single-point estimates that put too much emphasis on just one possible future course of events.

Using a range of forecast inputs to the mean-variance optimization process yields a large number of potentially optimal asset allocations.

Taking the median of these potentially optimal weights for each risk level yields a more robust approximation of the true optimal asset allocation. Because the resulting optimal asset allocation builds in many alternative ways the future may evolve, I believe that the risk estimation is more reliable. I also believe that the weightings are less extreme, more intuitive, and much more stable. Small changes to the estimate inputs typically lead to only small changes in the asset allocations. This reduces the need to make frequent and dramatic shifts in strategic asset class weightings. Instead, making asset allocation changes to reflect temporary changes in market conditions is done through tactical (as opposed to strategic) shifts in weightings, which I will discuss in detail in Chapter 9.

My recommended optimal asset allocation weightings are not meaningfully different from the market portfolio. The resulting asset class weights mirror the long-term average market-capitalization distribution of assets. The allocation to large-, mid-, and small-cap stocks reflects that the distribution of market cap among these asset capitalization ranges is around 85 percent, 10 percent, and 5 percent respectively. It makes sense that if the market itself is efficient (for the most part), investors as a whole have priced stocks to reflect the prospects for future returns and the resulting allocation of market assets among the capitalization ranges is efficient. See Figure 8.1.

Over time, the distribution of market cap appears to be consistent across capitalization ranges. Why is that important? It provides a stable basis for making tactical investment decisions. The capitalization breakdown of the universe of large- and small-cap stocks aligns closely with the large-cap S&P 1500, which encompasses the large-cap S&P 500, mid-cap S&P 400, and small-cap S&P 600. The capitalization distribution remained very stable throughout the late-1990s bubble.

It also is important to remember that the combined weighting of 15 percent of equity exposure in mid- and small-cap stocks reflects the fact that, most of the time, these stocks underperform their large- cap counterparts. As discussed before, only during the first third of the business cycle do they outperform. But what about that one-third? Chapter 9 will present the adaptive tactical framework that will enable investors to take advantage of small-cap performance in the early stages of the cycle, but minimize exposure for the remainder of the cycle and achieve the long-term target strategic allocation of 15 percent.

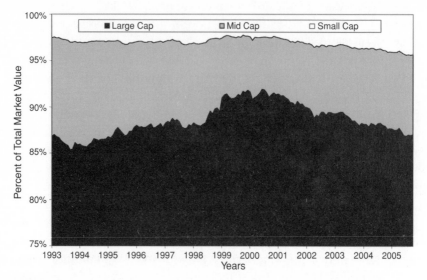

FIGURE 8.1   Total U.S. market size breakdown consistent over time.
Percentage of the U.S. stock market total market value across capitalization.

Asset Class Weightings by Geography

About 50 percent of the world's companies are domiciled outside of the
United States. Yet, only 20 percent of investable equity opportunities lay
outside of the United States. One reason for this is that foreign companies more typically finance their operations with debt (often from state-
controlled banks, like those in Japan and China). Another reason is that
the equity of many foreign companies is closely held by local families
and does not trade enough to be considered liquid. The result is that
global market capitalization (which represents actual investment opportunity) is skewed toward the United States.

To determine the available market capitalization of international
stocks to a U.S. investor, I use the following screening criteria.

■ The market capitalization of the company must be greater than the
$250 million micro-cap threshold.
■ To ensure appropriate liquidity, I use the standard definition of minimum liquidity, which is that at least one-third of the company's
outstanding shares must trade in a year.

■ The stock must be available to U.S.-based investors—some countries restrict foreign ownership. (For example, U.S. citizens cannot own Chinese A shares.)

The relationship of U.S. to international companies has remained fairly stable over time. Internationally domiciled companies historically represent 20 percent of total global market capitalization and U.S. companies make up the rest.

A 20 percent weighting also happens to be the optimal historical allocation when looking to minimize volatility in a portfolio. A higher strategic allocation to international equities has not proven to provide significant additional diversification benefits. See Figure 8.2

In a balanced asset allocation that contains a total equity weighting of 65 percent, allocating 20 percent of the total equity portion to international equities translates into a 13 percent overall weighting of the total portfolio in international equities (see Table 6.1).

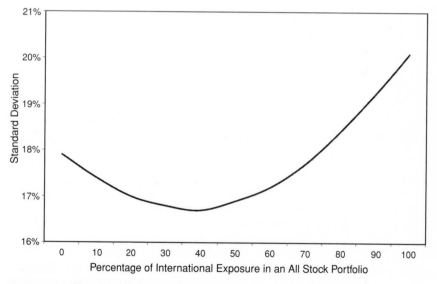

FIGURE 8.2   The impact of international investing on portfolio risk.
Volatility of combined U.S. and international equity portfolio based on different international stock weightings over past 20 years.

I separate the international market into asset classes consistent with the U.S. market—by style (growth/value) and market capitalization. First, I find this to be the most appropriate way to define asset classes given that size, style, and even sector correlations have risen across regions as global markets have become more integrated. In addition, more truly multinational corporations continue to emerge, and many have only modest exposure to any one country, even their country of domicile.

Secondarily, there are few benefits to allocating to international equities according to developed and emerging markets definitions. Emerging market stock opportunities are unique. Just one or two companies can dominate markets. Each company differs from the next in a large number of potential ways. Lack of stability, relative immaturity of financial markets, accounting and legal systems, political risks, liquidity, inefficiencies, low transparency, potential for corruption, and so on—they all must be considered when making emerging market investments. Therefore, committing to emerging markets should be done on a company-by-company basis.

International small-cap exposure is not a replacement for emerging markets exposure; they have very different performance profiles, illustrated by the low correlation, 0.44, between them.

Equity Asset Class Relative Weighting Consistent Across Profiles

The optimal baseline equity asset allocation is consistent across the six asset allocations (same proportion of large-, mid-, and small-cap for different asset allocations) because it is optimal (see Table 6.1). The ratio of return-to-risk would decrease if one made changes to the weightings across size, style, or geography.

To create a more aggressive asset allocation, it is better to maintain the optimal mix of equity asset classes and increase the overall equity allocation. For instance, if you simply added more small-cap exposure to an asset allocation instead of raising its overall equity exposure, the potential risk and return of the allocation would rise, but the potential increase in return would be less than what would result from a comparable increase in the overall equity weighting allocated in proportion to the strategic asset allocation.

The most efficient way to increase return potential and risk and is to raise the overall equity allocation while maintaining the same proportion among asset classes. It makes more sense to simply allocate more to stocks and keep the higher ratio of return-to-risk for the optimal mix of equity asset classes, rather than get incrementally less return relative to risk by increasing risk through allocating more assets solely to higher risk asset classes.

Fixed-Income Asset Classes

To establish a baseline for the fixed-income asset class weightings, I apply the same market-based principles that define the equity baselines. The fixed- income baseline is defined by the allocation of capital across the fixed-income market, as defined by the Lehman Aggregate Bond Index.

Currently, the average credit quality in the Lehman Aggregate index is AA+/AA1 and constitutes the baseline for credit quality. Similarly, the duration on the Lehman Aggregate Index is 4.5 years, and defines our baseline for duration. These allocations are reflected as an allocation of all strategic bond exposure to the core bond asset class, which mirrors the market exposure across duration and credit quality. Chapter 9 will present the tactical framework that will allow investors to take advantage of the other bond asset classes as market conditions warrant.

CHAPTER 9

Managing Risk Through Adaptation

To meet investment objectives, it is essential to manage the risk of the asset allocation on an ongoing basis. Investments fluctuate in value. In this chapter, I will present the tools and techniques to tactically manage the asset allocation to take advantage of market fluctuations to achieve the goals of your investment plan.

When investors talk about risk, we often discuss specific qualitative risk factors that we believe will affect financial markets. However, in the capital markets, risk is most often measured quantitatively as security price fluctuations—or volatility. Price volatility typically reflects investor uncertainty. It tends to fall as the economy is recovering from a recession and often rises as the business cycle matures. Shocks to financial markets, like the 1987 stock market crash or the 1998 Russian debt default, can result in temporary deviations from the cyclical pattern of volatility. Nevertheless, the midpoint of the business cycle often marks the turning point for volatility.

One often-cited proxy for the volatility of the stock market as a whole is the Chicago Board Options Exchange's Volatility Index, which measures the degree of volatility priced into stock index put and call options. Having fallen from elevated levels in the aftermath of the recession and lingering bear market, the Volatility Index has recently fallen in line with historical lows (see figure 9.1). One indicator that reflects bond market volatility is bond-rating agency Moody's speculative default rate.

117

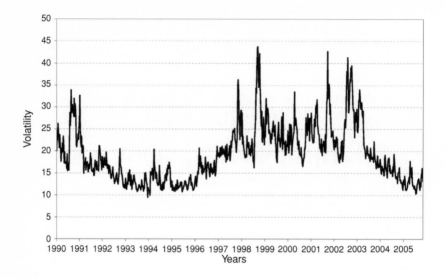

FIGURE 9.1 Implied volatility in line with historical lows.
CBOE Volatility Index.

As highlighted in Chapter 5, the stock market's volatility cycle and the business cycle are linked—volatility widens during periods of stress around recessions and narrows as conditions improve during recoveries. Bond market volatility also is linked to the business cycle because economic conditions affect changes in credit spreads. As the economy weakens, credit spreads widen to reflect the rising risk of default, and volatility increases.

Bond market volatility and the business cycle are also linked because of inflation. During the past 20 years, the month-to-month changes in consumer prices have exhibited twice the volatility around recessions than during expansions, and this has contributed to overall bond market volatility.

Because volatility is cyclical, the historical average of past volatility is not always the best predictor of future volatility in any given year. I believe we are at a turning point in the volatility cycle, with price volatility set to rise in the years ahead.

Why does rising price volatility matter? Because it feeds investor uncertainty as the business cycle matures, and creates opportunities to enhance performance. Most investors focus only on the negative aspects of volatility. However, I believe a more balanced perspective is appropriate. In fact, rising volatility presents more opportunities to manage risk and enhance return through tactical asset allocation. Rather than ignore volatility and adhere to a rigid allocation, the adaptive investor seeks to capitalize on market volatility through the flexibility of the market-based asset allocation framework.

To meet investment objectives, it is essential to manage the risk of the asset allocation on an ongoing basis. Does that seem daunting? If so, think of it this way: Choosing the amount of risk to take in a portfolio is one aspect of investing over which an investor actually has con-

Volatility and Diversification

In an environment of rising volatility, asset class correlation is a more meaningful determinant of overall portfolio returns. Correlation measures the degree to which asset returns move together or in opposite directions. Over time, the correlation between two asset classes can change. For instance, the relationship between the total returns of stocks and the total return of bonds has varied over the past 75 years. During much of the 1980s and 1990s, stock and bond prices generally moved together, as reflected in the relatively high +0.5 correlation between them over the period. In recent years, as in the 1950s, the correlation of stock and bond returns reversed, reaching −0.5.

I expect the correlation between stocks and bonds to rise modestly, but to remain below the levels seen in the 1980s and 1990s. Because bond prices fall as interest rates rise, lower correlation between stock prices and bond prices is the same as a high correlation between stock prices and bond yields. Given that I am forecasting a low and stable pace of inflation relative to historical levels, I believe that the volatility of interest rates may be driven more by expectations for the real rate of economic growth than by inflation expectations.

In general, rising inflation tends to be a negative for both stocks and bonds. In contrast, rising real growth is a plus for stocks but a negative for bonds, because bond yields generally rise (and bond prices fall). A similar period of negative correlation between stock and bond prices resulting from low and stable inflation occurred in the 1950s and 1960s. A lower-than-average correlation between bonds and stocks should produce more benefits from diversification, which should serve to moderate overall portfolio volatility.

trol. You cannot control the prices of securities at any point in time. But you can control the amount of risk you take by broadly diversifying at the asset class level, limiting the commitment to any single asset class, and managing risk over time by adjusting the allocations to asset classes as necessary with a disciplined approach. You achieve these adjustments through rebalancing and tactical risk management.

Rebalancing

Rebalancing is the process of periodically adjusting a portfolio to maintain the targeted asset allocation. Over time, one asset class may outperform another in a way that moves the allocation meaningfully away from the intended weights. To rebalance, sell some of the asset class that grew disproportionately and purchase an additional amount of the asset class that lagged. Rebalancing helps to keep the asset allocation on the road toward the long-term objectives. Rebalancing lowers risk and increases the likelihood of reaching your investment goals.

How often should you rebalance? For the sake of practicality, transaction costs, and tax efficiency, I believe it is most appropriate to rebalance annually or when any asset class has deviated 10 percentage points or more from your intended asset class target weighting. More frequent rebalancing, such as using 5 or 2 percentage point deviations or 3- or 6-month time periods as triggers for rebalancing, does not materially decrease risk. See Table 9.1.

The performance differences attributable to rebalancing are modest, but the reduction of risk is quite significant. It isn't surprising that reducing overexposure to an asset that has become relatively inflated and increasing exposure to a holding that has become proportionately smaller would lead to lower risk. What may be surprising, however, is the magnitude of the risk reduction. By my analysis, rebalancing a balanced portfolio on an annual basis would have reduced the maximum decline from −35 percent to −23 percent. In addition, a portfolio that is 80 percent stocks and 20 percent bonds (and has the recommended asset allocation consistent with our strategic weighting process discussed in Chapter 8) *and* is rebalanced is less risky—has been shown to have less volatility—than a 65 percent stocks/35 percent bond allocation that is not rebalanced.

TABLE 9.1   Benefits of a Rebalanced Asset Allocation

	Arithmetic Mean (%)	Standard Deviation (%)	Negative Periods	Average Decline (%)	Highest Return (%)	Lowest Return (%)	Maximum Decline (%)
Not Rebalanced							
Baseline Balanced	13.0	13.3	106	-4.5	9.7	-15.4	-35.0
10% Annual Rebalanced							
Baseline Balanced	13.2	11.8	102	-3.8	9.7	-15.4	-20.4
5% Annual Rebalanced							
Baseline Balanced	13.0	11.4	99	-4.0	8.8	-13.8	-22.0
2% Annual Rebalanced							
Baseline Balanced	12.7	11.4	101	-3.9	8.8	-13.8	-22.9
3 Month Rebalanced							
Baseline Balanced	12.8	11.3	101	-3.7	8.8	-12.1	-23.5
6 Month Rebalanced							
Baseline Balanced	12.7	11.3	100	-3.9	8.8	-12.6	-23.9
1 Year Rebalanced							
Baseline Balanced	12.8	11.4	100	-4.0	8.8	-13.8	-22.9

Disciplined management of the strategic asset allocation can help achieve lower volatility. With a greater degree of conviction to manage risk, you will have more certainty of achieving your investment goals.

Tactical Risk Management

You should rebalance your portfolio periodically to ensure it is aligned with the current recommended blend of asset classes. Doing so will preserve your intended level of risk exposure as market prices change. But what if market conditions or fundamentals change? Sometimes it may be prudent to temporarily (typically 6 to 36 months) reduce exposure to an asset class (or add exposure to an asset class not in your strategic allocation) when fundamentals change. This is called a tactical adjustment and is often done to reduce exposure to uncompensated risks.

Tactical risk adjustments go one step farther than strategic rebalancing. Tactical risk management generally involves shifts of up to ten percentage points in the weightings in the asset class components of the strategic asset allocation. Tactically adjusting approximately 10 percent of the portfolio has proven to be effective at managing risk and enhancing return, while remaining consistent with the original strategic allocation's risk and return profile. If an asset class is overvalued, and therefore subject to above-average likelihood of decline, the risk profile of the entire asset allocation will rise unless the investor makes an adjustment to preserve the intended level of risk.

Is tactical risk control the same thing as market timing? Absolutely not. Tactical shifts to overweight or underweight an asset class are based on a fundamental assessment of the outlook for that asset class. Market timing relies on charting technical strength (momentum) in an attempt to predict market price changes. Very few, if any, investors can accurately and consistently "time the market."

Naturally, some things are easier said than done. Without the right framework, it could easily become overwhelming to try to determine when and how to adjust asset allocation. In order to stay focused on what is most important, I first seek to tactically manage the risk of asset allocation among the weighting of stocks, bonds, and cash.

For example, the strategic allocation for a "balanced" portfolio may begin at a mix of 65 percent stocks/35 percent bonds/0 percent cash. If you determined that, for some period, stocks would offer less compensation for risk than bonds, you would tactically shift your balance port-folio allocation to a mix of 55 percent stocks/45 percent bonds/0 per-cent cash in an effort to preserve your intended risk profile. As the stock market risk rises, the potential for losses rises in an unmanaged asset allocation. If stocks are temporarily unattractive, it is likely that bonds are attractive. A shift of a portion of your portfolio from stocks to bonds—or any other shift among asset classes—accomplishes two things:

- The intended risk level of the allocation is maintained. Adapting the portfolio weightings as market conditions change keeps the portfolio on the road toward your investment goals; and
- If done effectively, the performance of the portfolio is enhanced by selling the overvalued asset and buying the undervalued one.

Why 10 percent shifts? Why not more? Adjustments in excess of 10 percent result in a material shift in the risk profile of the allocation and may result in a deviation from the strategically targeted return objective. In the prior example, the tactical shift called for a ten percentage point reduction in the portfolio's allocation to stocks and a ten-percentage-point increase in the allocation to bonds because we expected stocks to be temporarily unattractive relative to bonds. Then why not make a more dramatic shift out of stocks, say 20 percentage points? Or, better yet, an outright sale of all stock market assets? That is what market timing is all about, and remember, investors are rarely skilled at market timing. We would have no reason for any asset allocation or invest-ment plan if we always knew for sure which asset class would be the best or worst performer.

If a dramatic shift is done ineffectively, the performance of the port-folio could suffer. In reality, what this does is trade off something in which we have a high degree of confidence—that your strategic asset allocation will be successful in achieving your long-term investment goals—for something in which we can only have a lesser degree of con-fidence—the ability to consistently rotate out of the assets we are bet-ting will underperform and into those we are betting will outperform. Too much adaptation can be worse than too little.

In the context of a strategic allocation framework, a dramatic shift of more than ten percentage points changes the expected level of risk in the portfolio—from perhaps too risky to much too conservative to accomplish the objective of the strategic allocation. The forecast range of return and long-term performance objective becomes ineffective if the portfolio swings too broadly from the long-term target strategic asset allocation. Unless your life or financial circumstances change, your investment plan and your strategic allocation should not change just because of temporary market movements.

The six different strategic asset allocations detailed in Chapter 6 differ by 15 percent to 20 percent in their exposure to stocks and bonds. A shift of this magnitude goes beyond tactical risk management and instead changes a portfolio's long-term risk and return characteristics. In other words, a portfolio adjustment beyond ten percentage points is a shift of strategic allocation, not a tactical allocation shift. Therefore, the range of tactical risk management should remain contained within the boundaries that define the risk profile of your strategic asset allocation.

In addition to the stock/bond/cash allocation, tactical risk control can be used effectively to adapt the strategic asset allocation to market conditions in the three equity (size, style, and geography) and three fixed-income (duration, credit quality, and geography) asset classes.

Stock/Bond/Cash Tactical Risk Management

Stocks have outperformed bonds and cash equivalents most of the time in order to compensate investors for the additional risk associated with owning stocks. As detailed in Chapter 5, I believe that stocks will outpace bonds by about three to four percentage points a year, on average, over the next ten years. However, there are likely to be times when stocks do not provide enough return to fully compensate for their risk, relative to alternatives such as bonds or cash equivalents. Likewise, there may be times when the bond market does not provide adequate compensation for risk, relative to alternatives. At these times, tactical asset allocation becomes important to maintaining the intended risk profile of the asset allocation and remaining on the road to your investment objectives.

Since 1926, 26 percent of stock market and 8 percent of bond market returns were negative on a 12-month basis. However, only rarely—about 1 percent of the time—did both stocks and bonds post simultaneous year-over-year losses. Therefore, managing the stock/bond allocation can have a significant impact on the stability and predictability of portfolio performance.

Many factors contribute to a decision to make a tactical shift in the allocation between stocks and bonds, including the level of stock and bond market valuation, an assessment of unfolding economic conditions, the outlook for interest rates, trends in investor risk tolerance, and the forecast for corporate earnings growth.

Stocks are likely to outperform cash and bonds by more than the forecast average of three to four percentage-points when:

- The business cycle is in its early and middle stages.
- Stock market valuations are at or below the midpoint of the 14–19 range of the S&P 500 price-to-earnings ratio for the cycle.
- Short-term rates are falling.

Stocks are most likely to underperform bonds and cash when:

- Economic growth is falling during the late stage of the business cycle.
- Stock market valuations are at the high end of the 14–19 range of the S&P 500 price-to-earnings ratio for the cycle.
- Short-term interest rates rise above long-term interest rates.

Bonds are likely to perform well versus cash and stocks when:

- Economic growth is decelerating.
- Long-term interest rates are falling.
- Inflation is low.

Bonds are likely to underperform cash and stocks when:

- Long-term interest rates are rising from low levels.
- Economic growth is accelerating.
- Inflation is rising.

It is rare that cash is an attractive tactical alternative to stocks and bonds. It happens in an environment of high inflation, rising interest rates, slowing economic growth, and weakening corporate profits, such as occurred in the early 1970s. During 1973 and 1974, interest rates rose, inflation soared from 3 percent to 12 percent, the annual pace of infla-tion-adjusted economic growth slid from 7 percent to −2 percent, and profit growth slowed from near 30 percent to just single digits. Consequently, stocks tumbled as they discounted the ongoing slide in profits, and bonds suffered as inflation rocketed ahead. Yields on cash equivalents, such as the 3-month Treasury Bill, averaged more than 7 per-cent, lifted by inflation.

A tactical allocation to cash equivalents may be attractive when:
- Inflation is mounting.
- Short and long-term interest rates are rising.
- Economic growth is slowing.
- Corporate profits are weakening.

Equity Tactical Risk Management

Within your equity allocation, you can tactically manage the risk of the allocation with regard to the three categories of size, style, and geography.

Size

Over a full market cycle, total returns for large-, mid-, and small-cap stocks are likely to offer investors similar returns. Historically, small- and large-cap stocks have offered investors equivalent performance. In fact, since their inception in 1979, the large-cap Russell 1000 and small-cap Russell 2000 have provided average annual total returns that differ by only a few tenths of a percentage point.

Much like growth and value stock cycles, large- and small-cap stock performance tends to alternate around the broader market trend. The stocks of different-sized companies follow different patterns of perform-ance during the cycle, which can produce diversification benefits and opportunities for tactical risk control. As I pointed out in Chapter 5, early in a market cycle, small-cap stocks have typically outperformed large-caps by a wide margin. Investors generally embrace higher-risk small-cap stocks as the economy emerges from recession.

The current business cycle has reached the middle stage suggesting that the early cycle period of outperformance by small- and mid-cap stocks likely has ended, leaving these asset classes to underperform for the remainder of the cycle by an average margin of about 2–3 percent. After strong performance by small caps from early 2000 until early 2005, shifting to an underweight in mid- and small-cap stocks in favor of large caps for the remainder of the business cycle may be rewarding as the size cycle unfolds.

Remember, the strategic weighting of 15 percent of equity exposure in mid- and small-cap stocks reflects the fact that for most of a business cycle these stocks underperform their large-cap counterparts. The strategic weighting reflects this pattern of performance. In the early stage of the cycle, it makes sense to add another 10 percent of the portfolio value into mid- and small-cap stocks from large-cap stocks. In the middle stage, a baseline position will add diversification benefits. And, in the late stage, I recommend minimizing small- and mid-cap exposure to just 5 percent of equity. The tactical risk management of this asset class takes advantage of smaller-stock outperformance in the early stage of the cycle, then reduces exposure for the remainder of the cycle when the benefits of small- and mid-cap exposure are less, achieving the long-term target strategic allocation of around 15 percent.

What determines the size of the cycle? A major factor is the valuations and expected earnings growth of large-, mid-, and small-cap stocks relative to their historical relationships. In addition, the change in interest rates also affects the relative performance of capitalization ranges.

Conditions that favor large-cap stocks:

■ The business cycle is in its mature stages.

■ The pace of earnings-per-share growth is decelerating.

■ There is a cyclical rise in market volatility.

■ Interest rates are rising.

■ Valuations are falling.

■ Bond market credit spreads are tightening.

■ Dividends are growing at a strong pace.

Interest Rates and Size

When interest rates are rising, small-caps tend to underperform. This is due to the relatively higher valuations of small-cap stocks, and their greater sensitivity to financing conditions. In addition, the universe of small-cap stocks is dominated by interest-rate sensitive financial companies. Three industries—regional banks, real estate investment trusts, and thrifts and mortgage finance—account for 25 percent of the earnings of the small-cap Russell 2000 Index but only 8 percent of the large-cap Russell 1000 Index. During the past 25 years, when interest rates are rising by more than 50 basis points year-over-year, small-caps underperform their large-cap peers by an annualized 2.3 percent.

Conditions that favor small-cap stocks:

■ The business cycle is in its early stage.

■ The pace of earnings-per-share growth is rising.

■ There is a cyclical fall in market volatility.

■ The mergers and acquisitions environment is strong.

■ Interest rates are falling.

■ Bond market credit spreads are widening.

Style

As mentioned before, growth and value stocks offer similar performance over time, but one style tends to be in favor for a period of a few years—outperforming the other by an average of 8 percent on an annualized basis—and then this reverses as the other style comes into favor.

The most recent style cycle was record-breaking in magnitude. The high-flying growth stocks of the late 1990s gave way to value stock outperformance as the technology bubble burst. While both styles saw strong gains, growth stocks outperformed value stocks by an annualized eleven percentage points from mid-1994 until early 2000. Subsequently, value stocks outperformed growth from early 2000 until the end of 2005, by an annualized ten percentage points. Combining these periods the style cycle lasted ten years, which was an exceptionally long time. Furthermore, the average performance differential was wider than the normal eight percentage points.

In the new era of investing, I expect more muted style-relative performance differences over the remainder of the decade. Several factors support this view.

- Style composition is now more evenly distributed across cyclical and defensive industries than in the 1970s or 1980s when growth was dominated by the defensive consumer staples and health-care sectors.
- Although the value style has a slightly higher proportion of lower-quality companies (based on the Standard and Poor's Earnings and Dividend Rankings), the quality breakdown is more evenly distributed than in the past.
- Secular trends that would favor one style over another are not in place.

While the style cycle may offer less than the 8 percent historical average difference in performance, making tactical style allocations is still likely to provide opportunity to effectively manage risk and enhance return. It is still likely that the performance of the growth and value style will continue to oscillate. Thus, limiting exposure to an underperforming style could materially improve a portfolio's performance.

One tool that I use to tactically manage style exposure is based on the year-over-year price performance of the S&P 500. As the momentum of the year-over-year price changes in the S&P 500 peaks, the growth style typically begins to underperform. As S&P 500 momentum bottoms, the market typically begins its period of value underperformance. See Figure 9.2.

The reasons for the relationship between S&P 500 performance and the style cycle lay in the business cycle. Early in an economic recovery, low inflation and interest rates, as well as the rapid expansion of earnings, favor growth over value. Why? Because growth companies are less dependent on pricing power, have higher revenue and profit growth rates, and require attractive financing conditions to fuel growth. Later in the business cycle, S&P 500 price momentum historically has begun to fade (reflected not necessarily by declines in the Index level, but perhaps by just the pace of gains), earnings momentum has slowed, and

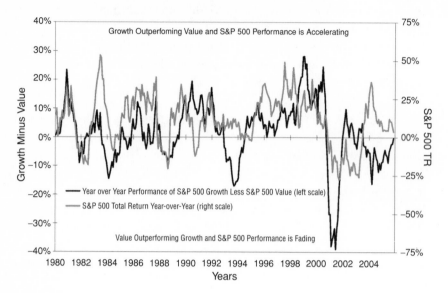

FIGURE 9.2 Style performance.
Year-over-year change in S&P 500 Growth less Value Index and S&P 500 total return.

interest rates have begun to rise. In response, investors have become more selective and typically favored a value orientation.

Over the past 25 years, following the simple guideline of S&P 500 year-over-year performance would have added 2 percent per year to an all-equity allocation by going entirely into growth (represented by the S&P 500 Growth Index) as momentum bottomed, and entirely into value (measured by the S&P 500 Value Index) as momentum peaked. Of course, such dramatic swings between growth and value may constitute too much adaptation and risk deviating from your investment plan. Limiting tactical style shifts to a maximum of 60 percent/40 percent split between styles would have added an average of 0.2 percent a year to return versus a static 50 percent/50 percent blend of styles.

Regardless of willingness to make large tactical shifts, the price momentum tool has worked historically. The next obvious question is: How does one forecast the momentum shifts? Unfortunately, the sector composition of styles has changed materially over time. Therefore, there is no perfect combination of factors that will consistently result in one style outperforming another. Some judgment is necessary in making a forecast of a turn in the style cycle. While relative earnings growth and valuation are contributing factors, the catalyst for a shift in the cycle is tied more typically to a shift in the macro environment, such as a sharp change in interest rates or economic activity. Most often, a number of factors must be in place to cause a shift.

Conditions that favor growth over value:
- Corporate profits as a percent of GDP are falling.
- Stock market valuations are rising.
- Merger and acquisition activity is rising.
- Interest rates are rising.
- Stock market volatility is rising.
- The pace of economic growth is slowing.
- Short-term interest rates are rising relative to long-term interest rates.

Conditions that favor value over growth:
- Stock market volatility is falling.
- Corporate profits as a percent of GDP are rising.
- Stock market valuations are falling.
- Interest rates are falling.
- Short-term interest rates are falling relative to long-term interest rates.
- The pace of economic growth is rising.

Geography

The relative performance of international stocks is affected by a number of factors, including currency, political and regulatory changes, and the global business cycle.

International stocks tend to be more value oriented than U.S. stocks. International markets have a much smaller amount of total market value concentrated in growth-oriented sectors, such as healthcare and information technology, and a much higher concentration in value-oriented sectors, such as financials, energy, utilities and materials. With a value orientation, international markets roughly track the style cycle—outperforming when value is in favor. See Figure 9.3.

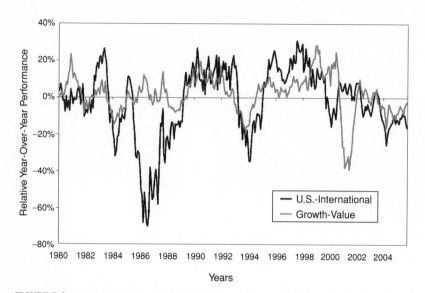

FIGURE 9.3   U.S. and international relative performance has tracked Growth and
              Value.
Year-over-year performance of S&P 500 less MSCI EAFE and S&P Growth less Value.

Given the value-bias, international stock performance has demonstrated more economic cyclicality than U.S. stocks. As the international
business cycle accelerates, international stocks have nearly always outperformed their U.S. counterparts. Over the past 30 years, there has
been only one period when international stocks underperformed U.S.
stocks as global economic indicators were rising from trough to peak.
That period was from April 1996 to July 1997, when the United States
was in the middle of a technology boom. Although international stocks
posted a respectable gain of 14 percent during that period, they were
unable to keep up with the stellar 50 percent gain in the S&P 500.

A simple strategy can be used to demonstrate the value that can be
added using this relationship. It involves allocating an additional 10 percent of your total asset allocation into international stocks (measured by
MSCI EAFE) when the year-over-year change in the index of leading
economic indicators for the Group of 7 countries (formed in 1976, this
group of seven leading nations includes: the United States, the United
Kingdom, France, Germany, Italy, Japan, and Canada) is rising, and
reducing exposure to international stocks by 10 percent of the total allo-

TABLE 9.2   International Stocks Outperform when Leading Indicators are Rising
Performance of S&P 500 and MSCI EAFE from Trough to Peak in Year-Over-Year
Change in G7 Index of Leading Indicators

Trough	Peak	Annualized Total Return		
		International	U.S.	Difference
Feb 78	Dec 78	38.3	18.8	19.5
Oct 82	Feb 84	37.7	17.9	19.8
Jan 87	Jan 88	15.0	−3.4	18.4
Nov 92	Dec 94	19.3	6.0	13.3
Apr 96	Jul 97	10.7	38.0	−27.3
Dec 98	Apr 00	15.2	14.8	0.4
Dec 01	Nov 02	−13.9	−18.7	4.8
Aug 03	May 04	32.7	17.0	15.7
Average		19.4	11.3	8.1

cation when G7 economic growth is declining. The average outperformance by international stocks from the trough to the peak in the G7 LEI is an annualized 8.1 percent. See Table 9.2.

Conditions that favor international stocks:
- Global economic growth is rising.
- The U.S. dollar is falling.
- Value stocks are in favor.

Fixed-Income Tactical Risk Control

Changes in market conditions may warrant an adjustment of risk exposures in the fixed-income portion of a portfolio on a tactical basis from the core bond weighting. For example, it may be advantageous to add high-yield bonds to a portfolio for a period of time, thereby temporarily lowering the overall credit quality, seeking to profit from improvement in business conditions. Alternatively, from time to time, it may be appropriate to add an allocation to government bonds to raise the overall credit quality of the bond allocation, in order to avoid losses due to deterioration in creditworthiness.

Credit Quality

To evaluate the outlook for risk and return with regard to credit quality, one can examine many factors, including historical yield spreads, default rates (see Figure 9.4), equity market volatility, merger and acquisition activity, U.S. business spending trends, and the movements in global credit ratings as measured by S&P and Moody's upgrade-to-downgrade ratio. Historically, when the upgrade-to-downgrade ratio has reached a peak, it has signaled the time to shift into higher-quality fixed-income instruments to insulate the asset allocation from potential losses and maintain the intended risk profile of the allocation. Correspondingly, when the upgrade-to-downgrade ratio has reached a nadir, it has typically been a signal that lower-quality debt will begin to outperform.

Using this indicator to tactically manage risk exposure across the spectrum of credit quality can effectively add value to an asset allocation. Over the 15 years that a liquid high-yield bond market has existed, simply allocating 10 percent of assets to high-yield bonds (represented

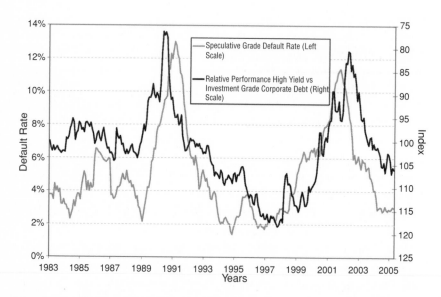

FIGURE 9.4   Credit quality cycle.
Speculative grade default rate and relative performance of high yield bonds.

by the Lehman High Yield Bond Index) from the core bond asset class when Moody's upgrade-to-downgrade ratio bottoms, and allocating 10 percent into Treasuries when the ratio peaks would have added 1.6 percentage points of return per year to the fixed-income portion of the asset allocation, or 0.6 percentage points of return per year to the overall performance of a 65 percent/35 percent balanced allocation.

Conditions that favor high yield bonds:

- Credit spreads are high and falling.
- Economic growth is rising.
- The profit cycle is in its early stage.
- The pace of capital spending relative to earnings growth is below average.
- The debt-to-capital ratio is low.
- Default rates are falling and the upgrade-to-downgrade ratio is rising.
- Stock market volatility is falling.

Duration

Changes in the outlook for interest rates are the key to tactical changes to duration. And an outlook for interest rates is made with an eye toward the overall strength of the economy, inflation metrics, and Treasury financing needs. However, the actions of the Federal Reserve always play a key role in any tactical duration shifts. Broadly speaking, when the economy is accelerating and the Fed is expected to raise its federal funds rate target, a tactical shift to lower duration (less interest-rate-sensitive) fixed-income instruments would be warranted to preserve value and maintain the intended risk profile of the allocation. Alternatively, when the economy is decelerating or expected to move into recession, inflation is falling, and the Fed is expected to ease monetary policy, a longer duration stance would be most prudent. You can adjust your portfolio's duration and manage interest-rate risk by incorporating an allocation to shorter- or longer-term bonds as necessary.

Effectively managing this risk can have a significant impact on the performance of the fixed-income asset allocation. For this type of tactical risk management, I have a simple rule related to Fed activity and using U.S. Treasuries to measure just the duration effect. It involves shifting to a short duration stance (using 1–3-year U.S. Treasuries as a proxy) over the entire period the Fed is raising interest rates or tightening monetary policy. Since 1974, there have been nine distinct periods of Fed interest rate hikes. Applying this simple rule has led to an outperformance over the baseline (measured by mid-duration Treasuries) by 2.6 percentage points. Furthermore, a short-duration portfolio during Fed tightening outperformed a portfolio invested entirely in long-dated fixed-income securities (approximated by 15-year or longer U.S. Treasuries) by an impressive 4.7 percent. For a balanced (65 percent/35 percent) portfolio, that 2.6-percentage-point fixed-income outperformance translates into 0.9-percentage-point performance improvement for the portfolio overall.

Conditions that generally favor long-term bonds relative to short-term bonds:

- Economic growth is slowing.
- Inflation is falling.
- Long-term interest rates are falling.
- The Fed is lowering the federal funds rate target.

Factors that generally favor short-term bonds relative to long-term bonds:

- Economic growth is rising.
- Inflation is mounting.
- Short- and long-term interest rates are rising.
- The Fed is raising the federal funds rate target.

Geography

In Chapter 6, I explained why international bonds do not qualify as a strategic asset class. For U.S.-based investors, the value of the dollar drives the performance of international bonds. As the dollar falls in value, interest payments on the international bond translate into more dollars, boosting total return. Thus, a tactical allocation to international bond funds that do not hedge their currency exposure may add value when the dollar is falling. On the other hand, as the dollar rises in value relative to the currencies in which foreign bonds are invested, the return is lowered as you convert the foreign-currency denominated interest payments you receive into fewer dollars.

Over the past 20 years, allocating 20 percent of bond exposure to unhedged international bonds when the dollar fell below its 12-month moving average would have yielded an excess return of nearly 1.75

Conditions that generally favor international bonds are those that place pressure on the U.S. dollar:

- A sharply rising U.S. trade and budget deficit.
- Rising U.S. inflation.
- A narrowing gap between U.S. and international short-term interest rates.
- Tightening global liquidity.

percentage points a year over U.S. bonds (measured by the Lehman Aggregate Bond Index) alone.

I presented my outlook for a depreciating dollar in Chapter 1. The series of crises in developing nations over the past ten years and the ensuing healing process has passed. Capital may now begin to flow back into developing nations. Developing nations' rising appetite for capital may lead to downward pressure on the dollar as these nations shift their savings from U.S.-dollar-based assets back into their own currencies to invest in internal economic infrastructure.

Ongoing Risk Management

The tools suggested for tactical risk control are elements in the process of managing the asset allocation. Nevertheless, many additional factors may influence your judgment. Ever-changing market dynamics (market evolution) make it necessary to constantly question relationships that may have worked in the past. They may not work in the future.

Tactical risk control involves the ongoing risk management of the asset allocation to reduce exposure to uncompensated risks (rather than purely to enhance return) while adhering to a long-term objective. In other words, the tactical adjustments are temporary risk-reducing departures from a strategically targeted path to achieve a long-term investment goal.

CHAPTER 10

Just the Facts

Now that you have an investment plan, a strategic asset allocation, and the tools to make tactical risk management decisions, the final thing you need is a way to find the data to help you make tactical decisions. The financial news media do a fine job of reporting the data, but you don't have to rely on them exclusively. Go straight to the source and get it for free—when you want it. This chapter focuses on what to look for, where to find it, and how to interpret it.

I have categorized the sources by the type of data they provide that is most useful to tactical decision-making. These sources include companies, trade associations, and government entities. All of the sources that I cite are independent, objective, and non-partisan in presentating the facts. The good news it that these sources produce a lot of data and you can learn all sorts of interesting facts. The bad news is that you could spend a lot of time fishing around until you find exactly what you want. In order to get you right to the particular information I reference when making tactical investment decisions, I have included links to specific webpages, not just the sources' Internet sites.

Business Cycle

The business cycle is very important to tactical decision making on the weightings in: Stocks/ Bonds/Cash, Size, Geography, Style, Bond Quality, and Duration. In fact, every tactical decision is in some way dependent upon the stage of the business cycle.

National Bureau of Economic Research
http://www.nber.org/cycles.html

The arbiter of the recessions and expansions of the business cycle is the National Bureau of Economic Research. While NBER typically does not establish a date for a recession until well after it is over, you can learn how long it has been from the last recession. This information is an important part of figuring out the current stage of the economic cycle. The data provided by NBER shows that business cycles are lasting longer, given increasingly effective inventory management and process improvements made possible by new technologies. I would expect a typical business cycle to last around ten years. NBER pegs the beginning of the current cycle at November 2001.

Bureau of Economic Analysis
http://www.bea.gov/bea/dn/home/gdp.htm

Another key source for economic cycle data is the Bureau of Economic Analysis. The BEA measures economic output and reports on the Gross Domestic Product each quarter. The BEA revises each quarterly GDP statistic multiple times as data becomes available but, even so, the report conveys a lot of information in the first release. The average pace of real, inflation-adjusted GDP is around 3.5 percent. If GDP is running above that, it can generate faster-than-average profit growth, but also higher inflation. Looking at the trend in real GDP growth can also be helpful in assessing the current stage of the economic cycle.

Organization for Economic Cooperation and Development
http://www.oecd.org

A good source for global economic data is the Organization for Economic Cooperation and Development. The OECD tracks indicators of economic performance for various regions of the world. It forms a composite index out of these many indicators to provide one all-inclusive indicator of economic activity. The outlook for global growth is more important to geographic tactical decision-making.

Inflation

Inflation is critical to tactical decision-making. Most importantly, inflation influences the weightings in Stock/Bond/Cash, Style, Size, and Duration. Rising inflation is bad news for financial investments because it erodes the value of future returns. However, a few years ago, concerns surfaced that inflation could also fall too low or even turn negative. The argument goes that negative inflation (a general decline in prices, also known as deflation) resulting from a collapse in demand is associated with slow economic growth, rising joblessness, and financial problems in the banking and corporate sectors. If the year-over-year pace of inflation measured by the Consumer Price Index strays out of a band of 2 to 4 percent and shows no sign of reversing, it may become worrisome to financial markets.

Bureau of Labor Statistics
http://www.bls.gov/cpi/home.htm

The Bureau of Labor Statistics produces the most widely used measure of inflation, the Consumer Price Index. The CPI measures inflation as experienced by consumers in their day-to-day living expenses.

The University of Michigan
http://research.stlouisfed.org/fred2/series/MICH/

The University of Michigan produces a widely watched survey of inflation expectations. However, the best place to find this information is not from The University of Michigan, but the Federal Reserve Bank of St. Louis. Expectations for inflation are important because they can be self-fulfilling. Workers who expect higher inflation may seek higher wage increases from their employers who, in turn, may then have to pass the cost onto customers. The result of this chain of events is inflation.

Federal Reserve

http://www.federalreserve.gov/fomc/

The Federal Reserve Board influences the availability and cost of borrowing, with the intention of promoting national economic goals. Eight times per year, the Federal Open Market Committee meets to determine the appropriate stance of monetary policy, and assesses the risks to its long-run goals of price stability (or low inflation) and sustainable economic growth. The outcomes of these meetings are market-moving because they often provide insight about the Fed's outlook for the economy and what steps they may take to influence the direction of inflation and economic growth. At 2:15 P.M. on the last day of the FOMC meeting, the Fed releases an official statement about the meeting. The statement typically consists of only a few carefully written paragraphs, but financial markets scrutinize each word. If the Fed intends to raise or lower their target for the federal funds rate, the statement will include their new target. Analysts also look for clues about the Fed's intended direction and magnitude of future interest-rate changes. The Fed releases more expansive minutes of the FOMC meeting a few weeks later. The meeting minutes provide much more information about the Fed's current thinking.

Earnings Growth

The outlook for earnings growth is most important to tactical adjustment of asset class weightings in Stocks/Bonds/Cash, Style, Size and Bond Quality. Over a full business cycle, a 7 percent rate of growth is likely but, in any given year, earnings can swing widely. Whether earnings are likely to rise or fall has a material impact on the performance of financial markets. Recall the saw-tooth pattern of earnings growth presented in Chapter 2. Knowing the current stage of the cycle provides much of what you need to determine where it is headed.

Institute for Supply Management

http://www.ism.ws/ISMReport/GraphicalDataIndex.cfm

One indicator of the outlook for earnings growth is the Institute for Supply Management Manufacturing Report on Business®. Each month, the ISM surveys more than 400 companies in 20 industries across the United States to compile its manufacturing purchasing manager index. This index has a high correlation with earnings growth. See Figure 10.1.

Federal Reserve
http://www.federalreserve.gov/releases/G17/Current/default.htm

Capacity utilization measures companies' percentage of operating capacity currently in use. It has been a good indicator of corporate profits. Why? Rising capacity utilization suggests output is rising, which may lead to improved profits. The relationship between capacity utilization and profit margins has been consistent for decades. As businesses use more of their productive capacity, they spread fixed costs over more units of output, in turn lowering their per-unit costs and raising profit margins.

This indicator may lose some of its usefulness in the future because the proportion of U.S. business devoted to manufacturing has been slid-

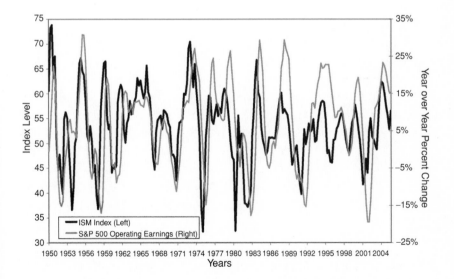

Figure 10.1   ISM Index a good proxy for S&P 500 operating earnings per share growth.

S&P 500 operating earnings year-over-year percent change in four quarter sum and Institute for Supply Management PMI Index.

ing for decades. Today, manufacturing industries employ only 10 percent of the U.S. workforce. However, manufacturing activity is itself a good barometer of what is happening in service-oriented businesses, so this indicator may still have some value in the years to come. See Figure 10.2.

Bureau of Economic Analysis
http://www.bea.doc.gov/bea/dn/nipaweb/SelectTable.asp

A tactical tool for determining the style tactical weighting is the ratio of corporate profits to GDP. However, you have to calculate this one yourself. Using the BEA's National Income and Product Account Table 1.14, entitled, "Gross Value Added of Domestic Corporate Business in Current Dollars and Gross Value Added of Nonfinancial Domestic Corporate Business in Current and Chained Dollars," divide line 12 by line 1. As I

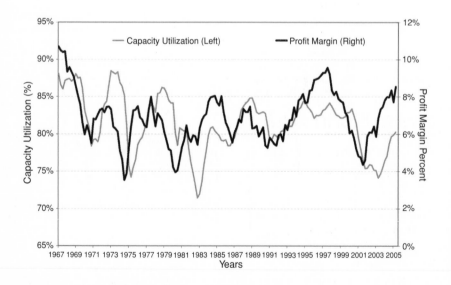

FIGURE 10.2   Profit margins sensitive to capacity utilization.
Profit margin of non-financial corporations and capacity utilization.

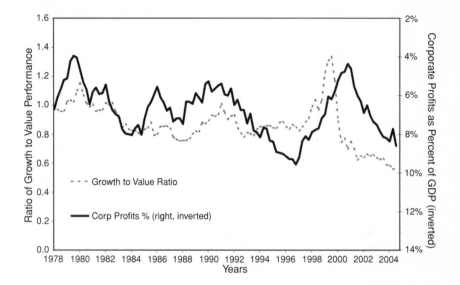

FIGURE 10.3 Relative performance of Growth and Value and corporate profits as percent of GDP.

S&P 500 Growth Index divided by Value Index and non-financial corporate profits divided by nominal GDP.

point out in Chapter 9, when this percentage is falling it favors growth, and when it is rising it favors value. See Figure 10.3.

Credit Quality and Interest Rates

The outlook for credit quality and interest rates are the two main ingredients to tactical asset class weightings for bonds.

Moody's Investors Service

http://www.moodys.com/default.asp

Moody's, a global bond-rating agency, is a top source for credit quality measures. You can use credit trends and default rates to help determine your appropriate exposure to high-yield bonds. Improving credit trends typically coincide with a recovering economy in the early-to mid-stages of the business cycle.

Congressional Budget Office
http://www.cbo.gov/publications/bysubject.cfm?cat=35

The Congressional Budget Office produces cost estimates for every bill reported by a Congressional committee. The CBO also produces a number of budget-related reports, including the Monthly Budget Review, which provides a current analysis of the Federal budget summarizing the fiscal activity of the government during the previous month. The CBO is a great resource for assessing the impact of the Federal government's borrowing needs and the potential impact on interest rates.

PART III

Investing
in the New Era

Parts 1 and 2 presented the evolutionary changes that are resulting in a new era of investment performance and a new approach to investing that incorporates an adaptive, market-based framework for achieving goals in the coming years. This section explores how to adapt by using alternative investments, changing the age-old approach to style, and implementing your investment plan in the new era of investment performance.

We live in a world of relentless innovation. New, alternative investments are changing the way we approach asset allocation. Investments with unique characteristics unlike those of traditional investments may provide valuable diversification.

The financial markets are continually evolving and investment strategies must adapt to the changing environment. This applies not only to the differences in asset-class performance and inter-relationships, but also to the asset classes themselves. Investment style, defined as growth and value, may reflect increasingly out dated characteristics. A new approach to style may become necessary as the style constituents evolve.

As markets evolve, the best way to implement an investment portfolio may change. In the new era of investment performance, an active approach may be more rewarding than during the passive, buy-and-hold period of the 1990s. A mix of both active and passive investment vehicles may be the best way to implement the asset allocation in the years ahead.

This section prepares you for the future through the adaptation and implementation of the market-based portfolio. Chapter 11 incorporates alternative investments into the strategic asset allocation, including private equity, volatility (including hedge funds), private real estate, natural resources, and infrastructure. Chapter 12, predicts an evolution in the way the markets define asset-class style: from growth and value, to defensive (high quality) and cyclical (low quality). Finally, armed with all the tools to construct your asset allocation, Chapter 13 focuses on how to implement the strategies presented in this book.

CHAPTER 11

Alternative Investments

When many investors hear the term, "alternative investments" they think of hedge funds. True, hedge funds are a type of alternative investment. But there is a much broader universe of alternatives to more traditional investments (such as stocks and bonds). Actually, some alternative investing techniques use traditional investments in non-traditional ways. A little confusing? It is best to think of alternative investments in two separate groups:

- Assets that are sold privately and are relatively illiquid. This category includes investments in private equity, private real estate, natural resources (such as oil and gas or timberland partnerships), and infrastructure (such as toll roads and bridges).
- Traditional assets purchased using non-traditional investing strategies. Hedge funds fall into this category, as does "volatility."

Each alternative investment offers unique performance characteristics that differ not only from traditional asset classes but also from other alternative investments. From this perspective, there are five major categories of alternative investments.

- Private equity refers to the ownership shares of companies that are not listed on a public stock exchange. Companies raise funds through private equity offerings for many of the same reasons that public companies issue stock—to expand working capital, to make acquisitions, or to strengthen their balance sheet. Companies of any size or at any stage of development may issue private equity.

■ Private real estate, like private equity, involves the purchase of real estate directly through property pools, commingled real estate funds (CREFs), syndications, or separate accounts that are managed by professional real estate portfolio managers or investment advisors. In general, these invested assets are used for property development or renovation.

■ Natural resources refers to domestic and international investments in timber, direct oil and gas assets, and oil and gas private equity partnerships.

■ Infrastructure investments involve private financing of public transportation infrastructure such as roads, bridges, airports, and public transit systems. These investments may take a number of forms, most commonly private-partnership-owned leases on new and existing infrastructure.

■ Volatility and hedge funds relate to investment strategies that are generally correlated with volatility. Volatility exposure can be obtained through the futures and swaps markets. Hedge funds are generally sold in private placement transactions and are often organized as limited partnerships or limited liability companies.

Investing in Alternatives

On the surface, alternative investments seem to provide very high risk-adjusted returns compared to traditional asset classes. However, conventional methods of assessing the attractiveness of an asset class as part of an overall investment portfolio—historical correlation, volatility, and returns—have significant shortcomings relative to more traditional assets.

Why? To begin with, the data set that represents the alternative investment universe is not complete. Like the universes of traditional asset classes, it suffers from what is commonly known as "survivorship bias." As poor performers discontinue operations, they drop out of the universe and index performance calculations; thus performance statistics can be artificially biased upward. Furthermore, index statistics do not contain the performance data of all active market participants; some alternative investment managers seeking to maintain exclusivity and privacy may not submit information to databases and index providers.

Another problem stems from the fact that alternative investment returns do not reflect the market's illiquidity and infrequent pricing. For instance, standard deviation is a quantitative statistic traditionally used to measure the risk of an asset class. Standard deviation measures price volatility; if the investment is illiquid and lacks frequent pricing, the statistic is not very meaningful. The distribution of returns for alternative investments, which is far from normal, also weakens the usefulness of standard deviation as a measure of risk. Risk, measured by volatility, is biased downward artificially for alternative investments.

In contrast to traditional investments, the valuation of illiquid investments is subject to several unique factors.

- Managers estimate values. They are not determined by market forces, as in the public markets.
- Managers calculate values infrequently. This lack of liquidity masks the investments' underlying volatility.
- Because of the risky nature of private investments, losses may be concentrated in the earlier years.

For these reasons, the true performance of an illiquid investment can only be estimated and not determined definitively until the investment is exited.

How do you overcome these limitations in order to analyze alternative and conventional investments together? One way that I believe provides meaningful results is to determine the true economic and fundamental drivers of asset returns. Over the past 20 years, the most significant negative outcomes for alternative investments were the result of an unexpected event, such as the 1998 Russian debt crisis and the Long Term Capital Management hedge fund debacle. Therefore, risk for alternative investments should be defined more subjectively. One way is to represent risk as the potential for relationships to change suddenly. To that end, you must analyze alternatives in the context of many possibilities, such as what would happen if:

- Correlations change.
- A regional currency crisis erupted.

■ The relationship between shorter- and longer-dated volatility changes dramatically.

■ A major bankruptcy or downgrade occurs and causes a dramatic and sudden widening of credit spreads.

The performance of alternative investments varies more widely within the same category than traditional investments. Given that there are both quantitative and qualitative dimensions to risk assessment, a thorough understanding of the terms and characteristics of an alternative investment vehicle is very important. Most offerings are unregulated because the people investing in them are very sophisticated, wealthy investors, who meet the Securities and Exchange Commission's definition of an "accredited investor." Often, alternative investment vehicles are limited to a maximum of 100 investors.

In order for an individual to qualify as an accredited investor under the SEC's Regulation D, which governs private placement exemptions, they must meet one of the following expectations:

■ Earn an individual income of more than $200,000 per year or a joint income of $300,000 in each of the last two years, and expect to reasonably maintain the same level of income.

■ Have a net worth exceeding $1 million, either individually or jointly with their spouse.

■ Be a general partner, executive officer, director, or a related combination for the issuer of the security being offered.

Each alternative investment vehicle is unique and has some limitations. In general, however, the broad categories of alternative investments do add value to a strategic allocation. A qualified investor with a balanced asset allocation and a tolerance for some illiquidity may, in an effort to improve the reward/risk relationship, include a 20 percent allocation to alternative investments (10 percent for conservative investors, and as much as 30 percent for aggressive investors).

The strategic asset allocation weightings presented in Chapter 8 are scaled down proportionately to accommodate an allocation to private equity. Thus, for qualified investors, the baseline balanced asset allocation could be defined as:

- 50 percent in public stocks.
- 30 percent in bonds.
- 5 percent in private equity.
- 10 percent in private real estate.
- 3 percent in hedge funds and volatility.
- 2 percent in natural resources.

This reflects the 80 percent of the total portfolio invested in traditional asset classes with an adjustment to the public-equity exposure. This maintains the intended risk profile of the balanced asset allocation.

Achieving allocation targets with publicly traded traditional investments is straightforward. Maintaining somewhat precise allocations is also achievable because one can rebalance as needed. However, when including alternative investments, you must view target allocation percentages more broadly. Why? First, it may not be possible to employ a full allocation to an alternative investment at one time—private transactions are frequently funded in stages. Second, with illiquid alternative investments, rebalancing can be very difficult. Therefore, it is not practical to consider one optimal allocation to an alternative investment. Rather, consider a range of appropriate allocations. I will recommend target allocations to alternative investments within a range.

It is important to note that weightings in alternative assets are part of a strategic, long-term portfolio allocation. They are not temporary, tactical allocations. Commitments usually last about ten years.

I will discuss the merits and risks of each alternative investment category individually.

Private Equity

Private Equity refers to ownership shares of companies that are not listed on a public stock exchange. Companies raise funds through private equity offerings for many of the same reasons that public companies issue stock—to expand working capital, to make acquisitions, or to strengthen their balance sheet. Companies of any size or at any stage of development may issue private equity. Once an investment is made, it is generally very illiquid. Transferring or selling an ownership interest in private equity is much more difficult than selling a publicly traded stock. In the absence of a marketplace or exchange, an investor who wishes to sell ownership interest in a private company must find a buyer. More often than not, investors exit their private equity investment when one of four things occurs:

- The company is sold to or merges with another company.
- The company is sold to another group of investors.
- The company's stock is offered on a public exchange through an Initial Public Offering (IPO).
- The company recapitalizes (changes the structure of its balance sheet).

Because of their illiquid nature, private equity investments tend to be long-term investments.

Financial investments in private companies were once done through Small Business Investment Corporations. After a series of tax and pension law changes in the late 1970s, limited partnerships became the predominant vehicle for investing in private equities. In a limited partnership fund, investors become limited partners and make a commitment to contribute capital to the partnership. A professional investment manager typically acts as the general partner and is responsible for deploying the fund's capital by identifying, evaluating, and making direct investments in many private companies (referred to as "portfolio companies" once an investment is made). General partners typically make a capital contribution to the partnership.

Once established, a private equity fund generally has a fixed life span of approximately 10–15 years. However, investors' committed capital (the amount that they have agreed to invest) will not be invested in the fund for its entire life span. The general partner will arrange the fund's first closing. At that time, limited partners will invest a portion of their committed capital. Later, as the general partner identifies investment opportunities, the general partner will request that limited partners invest more of their committed capital. General partners make capital calls over time, though most occur within the fund's first seven years. Consequently, investors make investments over time and may not reach a fully committed position for many years. Under certain difficult or competitive investing conditions, a fund's general partner may not call for the full committed amount during the life of the fund.

When a fund exits a portfolio company investment, the general partner distributes the proceeds to the investors. This can begin to occur even before the private equity fund has made all of its intended capital calls. In short, committed capital rarely equals invested capital. Therefore, investors may want to consider their allocation to private equity as a targeted average investment over the life of the commitment. As such, their capital commitment would exceed their targeted average exposure. A 5 percent target may entail exposure in a range of 2 percent to 10 percent over the course of the investment. See Figure 11.1.

Across the performance quality spectrum, private equity fund managers tend to specialize in certain types of investments, just as public equity managers do. Portfolio company characteristics often determine specialties. These characteristics include size, life-cycle stage, industry, product or service set, and geographic location domestically and/or internationally. Generally, private equity investing falls into two broad strategy categories: venture capital and corporate finance.

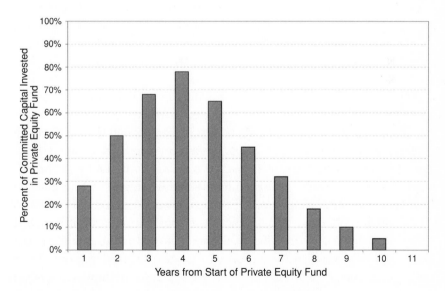

FIGURE 11.1   Typical called capital schedule for private equity.
Percent of committed capital invested in private equity fund.

■ Venture capital is money provided to private companies very early in their life cycle, including start-ups. These companies tend to be very small in terms of employees and capital; they also lack the operating history or assets needed to obtain financing from banks. In general, the earlier in the life cycle of a company the greater the risk. Venture capitalists are willing to take on this risk when they can identify early-stage companies that have exceptional growth potential. They often expect high rates of return from their investments to compensate for additional risk.

■ Corporate finance generally describes investments in companies beyond the start-up, or early stage of development. This includes middle-stage companies and even mature, established companies. Portfolio companies can use capital for several purposes, including expansion of operations or restructuring of the companies finances. However, the most common type of private-equity financing is a buyout. A buyout occurs when an existing company buys all or part of another company. If a significant portion of the buyout is financed with debt, the deal is called a "leveraged buyout" (LBO). Nearly 70 percent of private equity investments are LBOs. If the existing management is part of the buying group, the deal is known as a "management buyout" (MBO). Often, buyouts are facilitated through a funding arrangement known as "mezzanine financing" that includes subordinated debt and an equity-like component.

With the introduction of the limited partnership structure in the 1970s, the private equity market grew dramatically. In the 1980s, a change in government regulations permitted pension funds to invest in private equity. The 1980s also marked a period of notoriety for private equity investing due to several, high-profile leveraged buyout partnerships. These partnerships bought companies and restructured them by eliminating ineffective and inefficient managers, aggressively cutting costs, and employing new technologies in order to improve performance. The partnerships then profited by selling the restructured company in an IPO or selling the assets of the company to another company.

In the 1990s, the market's emphasis turned from leveraged buyouts to venture capital. The technology boom created opportunities for partnerships to fund start-ups—sometimes with not much more than a good idea—and then profit through an IPO not long after.

The use of financial leverage will likely define this decade's wave of private equity. Companies generally carry much less debt in their capital structure than would be optimal to maximize earnings-per-share growth and, in recent years, U.S. public companies have actually been paying down their debt. However, aggregate corporate debt levels are on the rise. How can that be? Because the debt of private companies is rising. Enticed by low interest rates and an abundance of capital, many private equity firms are seeking under-leveraged companies and increasing the proportion of debt in their capital structures in an attempt to boost returns on equity.

The private equity market is essentially illiquid and has historically been inefficient. This combination has enabled skilled managers to achieve rates of return that exceeded those of the public markets. However, the private equity market is becoming more efficient for three key reasons:

- A growing secondary market for private equity limited partnership interests. In private-to-private deals, firms are now trading partnership interests with each other. In order to transact a deal, the parties must negotiate a price. To establish a fair price, the buyer and seller must have access to accurate and timely information. Thus, a secondary market improves efficiency and increases liquidity.
- Increasing use of auctions to sell a company or division. Traditionally, when a company wanted to sell a division, it approached one LBO firm. Today, it is increasingly likely that such a sale will occur through an auction, among multiple private equity firms. This competition for deals is increasing the efficiency of private equity.
- Hedge funds competing with private equity firms for the purchase of corporate assets. This adds another dimension of competition, and thus efficiency, to the market. I do not believe, however, that a convergence of hedge funds and private equity funds is occurring. The skills needed to extract value from a private company are very different from the skills needed to extract trading/arbitrage opportunities from publicly traded securities.

In short, private equity—once a very inefficient, relationship-driven market—has now turned into a more efficient, auction-driven market.

This greater efficiency leads to a rise in observed volatility. Why? An increase in a market's efficiency often occurs when the flow of information about the market improves. Historically, very little information was available about the private transactions occurring within the private equity market. In other words, private equity lacked transparency. Private equity investors were often unable to obtain accurate and current valuations of their direct portfolio company investments or of their limited partnership interests. Although most investors assumed that the underlying investments in a private equity fund were generally riskier than public equities, the lack of transparency made it difficult to observe the volatility. A growing secondary market and auction-driven transactions help to increase the amount of information available regarding the true value of private equity investments at any point in time. Thus, observed volatility is increasing.

Greater efficiency generally leads to lower investment returns. Why? As markets become more efficient, they tend to attract more participants—both investors and investment managers. More participants typically bring more capital into a market, and that capital must be deployed. As competition (demand) for private equity deals increases, investment managers may be forced to lower their required return expectations in order to deploy capital.

Two other considerations regarding the outlook for private equity performance involve credit spreads and changes in pension accounting. There has been a strong relationship between the performance of private equity investments and credit spreads (the difference in yield between U.S. Treasury debt securities and riskier non-Treasury securities with similar terms). Credit spreads are a way to measure the cost of capital: as spreads widen, capital becomes more expensive. The success of a portfolio company is usually very dependent on its ability to access inexpensive funding. As financial conditions ease (credit spreads narrow), private equity firms tend to do well; when conditions reverse, they tend to suffer. Currently, credit spreads are very narrow. Capital remains abundant, credit is relatively cheap, interest rates remain low, and borrowing terms are favorable. While these conditions may not deteriorate significantly in the near term, they may not continue to improve. This could begin to negatively affect the performance of private equity investments in the next few years.

However, a potential short-term positive for private equity performance involves changes in pension accounting rules being debated in Washington. Proposed changes would require pension plans to use current market prices to value (mark-to-market) their portfolio assets, rather than spread (smooth) gains and losses over several periods. A mark-to-market approach would increase the observed volatility of a plan value. In a declining market, a company would be at greater risk for having to make an unplanned contribution to their pension plan, which would negatively affect reported earnings. On average, large pension funds currently have an allocation to private equity investments of about 5 percent. Market-value accounting may induce some plans to shift more of their assets out of public markets and into private markets, where the values of infrequently priced assets tend to be smoother by nature of their illiquidity. Therefore, the demand for assets with the superficial appearance of being less volatile, such as private equity, may increase in the next few years. This could drive up the value of private companies.

During the past 20 years, net returns on private equity have exceeded returns in the public market (as represented by the S&P 500) by approximately 100 basis points on an annualized basis. This reflects an average across *all* of the strategies and styles within the private equity market. However, it is very important to understand that the performance among subcategories has varied considerably at times, with some subgroups significantly underperforming and others significantly outperforming the average.

In the future, will private equity outperform public equity on average? I have analyzed the drivers of performance for private equity, as well as the historical excess returns in private equity. I have analyzed all forms of private equity investing in the proportions represented in the overall universe of private equity funds. I expect greater efficiency in the private equity market resulting from an increase in secondary transactions, auctions, and competition. I also expect the outlook for private equity to reflect an overall trend toward lower returns across all investments.

Given those expectations, will private equity outperform public equity on average? First, I expect that average future returns for private equity will lag private equity returns of the past. Second, I expect that private equity returns will be slightly superior to the public equity markets, averaging about 50–100 basis points per year higher. Given a long-term total return expectation of 9 percent for public equities, my long-term total return forecast for private equities is 9.5–10.0 percent on an annualized basis.

For the most part, private equity investments have unique performance characteristics that are more like small-cap stocks than other alternatives, such as hedge funds (volatility), natural resources, or private real estate. A private equity investment in a certain industry or country may perform in a similar manner to smaller public companies in that industry or country. The tightness of this relationship will depend upon the specific investment employed.

A unique approach is necessary when assessing the risk and correlation for private equity. To compare private equity to public equity, most studies adjust the private equity market for liquidity and other data biases to put on par with the public markets. This approach entails many questionable assumptions. To overcome some of these problems, I take the public markets and put them on par with the private markets to create a Public-to-Private Market Equivalent ("P/PME").

To simulate the private equity market using S&P 500 data, I measured five-year time periods, due to the typical pattern of investment returns for private equity where capital typically starts to be returned in year five. To calculate the P/PME for every period, I used the purchase price of the index five years earlier, dividends during the five-year period to represent accumulated cash flows, and level of the S&P 500 at the end of the five-year period. The result is data to measure private equity and public equity correlation, and volatility, on a similar basis.

Comparing the data starting with the first quarter of 1986, the earliest date for which reliable data is available for private equity returns, I found that the correlation between the private equity market and the P/PME was around 0.9. It is intuitive that private equity and public equity correlation would be high, rather than the low or even negative relationship produced by other approaches to the data. One reason the correlation with the public market is high is that LBOs—which make up about 70 percent of private equity investments—are effectively leveraged public equities. Using the P/PME, the true underlying volatility of private equity is about twice as high as the volatility of public markets.

In contrast, traditional analyses of private equity that use unadjusted data series produce volatility measures which are generally half that of public markets.

This approach overcomes the smoothing effect that results from the infrequent pricing and lack of liquidity in the private equity market. Furthermore, the results are more reflective of the increase in observed private equity volatility occurring as liquidity and efficiency improve. These results are also better aligned with the greater volatility that small-cap U.S. stocks (as represented by the Russell 2000 Index) have displayed relative to large-cap U.S. stocks (as represented by the S&P 500).

I conclude that a target allocation of 5 percent, within a range of 2 percent to 10 percent, is appropriate for a balanced asset allocation. A slightly higher allocation for an aggressive investor and a lower allocation for a conservative investor—proportional to overall stock market exposure—would be appropriate. This allocation is based on the following attributes of private equity:

- High correlation with public markets.
- Higher risks associated with portfolio company volatility.
- Lack of liquidity in partnership interests.
- Lower expected risk-adjusted return than in the past.

For a balanced allocation, the recommend target weight of 5 percent of the total asset allocation represents about 8 percent of the equity portion. This allocation target and range are consistent with the market-based framework for portfolio weightings among traditional asset classes —private equity represents approximately 8–10 percent of the combined market value of all public and private equity.

Private Real Estate

Private real estate refers to the purchase of real estate directly through property pools, commingled real estate funds (CREFs), syndications, or separate accounts that are managed by professional real estate portfolio managers or investment advisors. In general, these invested assets are used for property development or renovation.

Data on the private real estate markets suffers from the same problems as private equity: poor liquidity, incomplete representation, and

REITS

Interests in real estate investment trusts (REITs) do not fall into the private real estate category. Some people classify REITs as real estate, but they are really equities in a specific industry within the public equity asset class. The REIT industry makes up 0.6 percent of the market value of the U.S. stock market represented by the S&P 1500 Supercomposite (encompassing the large-cap S&P 500, the mid-cap S&P 400, and the small-cap S&P 600 Indexes). The performance of REITs differs from direct ownership of real estate. In fact, REIT performance has no statistical relationship—or a zero correlation—with direct private real estate investment.

lack of efficient pricing. Appraisals drive the performance of private real estate, not actual transactions. As a result, the returns are smoothed over time and understate the underlying volatility.

Using the approach for assessing the relative volatility described in the private equity section, along with relevant academic research adjusting for appraisal lag and smoothing effects, my forward-looking estimate for the volatility of direct real estate is 8 percent to 10 percent. This estimate is higher than that of the unadjusted historical data. My 8–10 percent volatility estimate for private real estate is lower than my 14–18 percent volatility estimate for the public stock market, but higher than my 4–6 percent forecast for the bond market (both are presented in Chapter 5).

Unlike private equity, the correlation between the performance of private real estate and P/PME discussed in the private equity section is very low, at just 0.2 percent. Private real estate is also relatively uncorrelated with bond market performance. In fact, it correlates very highly with the pace of inflation. This suggests that private real estate is a very attractive portfolio diversifier—performing independently from the stock and bond markets, and acting as an effective hedge against inflation.

Private real estate is likely to offer investors a total return of 7.5 percent over the next ten years. This is above the return expectation for the bond market, but below that of the stock market. Interestingly, I believe the performance of private real estate is not eroding to the same extent as private equity. Private real estate has high barriers to efficiency—local knowledge is essential for valuation.

Private real estate performance has a high correlation to the pace of inflation and a relatively consistent inflation-adjusted return of about 5 percent. I believe that private real estate can maintain the historical return differential over the pace of inflation. A 5 percent inflation-adjusted return combined with the estimated pace of inflation of around 2 to 3 percent, results in a 7.5 percent annualized long-term nominal return forecast for private real estate.

I conclude that a target allocation of 10 percent, within a range of 5 percent to 20 percent, is appropriate for a conservative, balanced, or aggressive allocation, given the low correlation with both stocks and bonds. A 20 percent commitment of capital may be required and result in varying exposure over the course of the investment. This allocation is based on the following attributes of private equity:

- Even after adjusting for liquidity, private real estate offers a very low correlation with traditional and alternative investments.
- Effective barriers to efficiency are likely to maintain high-risk adjusted returns.
- Private real estate acts as an effective inflation hedge.

Compared to all other alternative investments, private real estate provides the most enhancement to a portfolio of traditional asset classes.

Natural Resources

Natural resources refers to domestic and international investments in timber, direct oil and gas assets, and oil and gas private equity partnerships.

The main factors that affect timberland performance are land and product price changes (timber sales, land sales and lease-income-generated returns). Another factor is biological growth (since trees become more valuable as they grow); inventory appreciates while it awaits a favorable market. Risks include not only the fluctuation in timber and land prices (and the illiquidity of the investment), but also losses associated with fires, storms, insects, and disease. Another risk is the potential for legislative or regulatory changes, such as those governing endangered-species and carbon dioxide emissions (there are developments related to carbon trading and emissions registration occurring at an international level, at a national level and at a local level). Alternative investments in timberland combine some of the aspects of private equity, private real estate, and commodities. However, timberland has had a low correlation with other investments (although data is very limited). The timberland market is not liquid, leading to potential market inefficiencies.

Direct oil and gas participation provides exposure to a share of the income generated by wells, in the form of monthly revenue checks. There may be tax benefits for some individuals—investors receive income without income taxes being deducted, and a direct participating investor may be entitled to tax deductions. Risks include the possibility of the loss of a portion, or all, of the investment principal if the well is unsuccessful.

It is difficult to generalize performance for this group of alternative investments; performance for each investment may vary widely and the data are subject to the same distortions as other alternative investments. Over the past 19 years that data are available, natural resources represented by timberland have offered investors returns modestly above those of the public equity markets, on average. While observed volatility is relatively high for a private investment, the underlying volatility is much higher. Using the approach for assessing the relative volatility described in the private equity section, timberland displays several times the volatility of that of the stock market P/PME. However, this investment provides significant risk diversification, given low correlations with public stock and bond markets and other alternative investments. In fact, timberland has provided a negative correlation with private real estate. Oil and gas returns also offer low correlations, but performance varies too widely to generalize.

A target allocation of 2 percent, within a range 0 percent to 5 percent, is appropriate for a balanced or aggressive investor, given the low correlation with both stocks and bonds.

Infrastructure

Over the next ten years, federal and state governments are likely to look to the private sector for help in financing public transportation infrastructure, such as roads, bridges, airports, and public transit systems. Infrastructure spending relative to economic growth has reached an all-time low even as traffic congestion continues to climb. Government budgets are already stretched thin and many communities are unwilling to raise taxes to fund infrastructure improvements. As a result, changes in legislation directed toward the private funding of new infrastructure projects are occurring across the United States. Many government authorities are seriously considering offering private leases on existing infrastructure to ease budget burdens.

Within the past couple of years, several infrastructure investments have actually taken shape in the United States:

■ In a first-of-its-kind transaction, private investors purchased a 99-year lease on the Chicago Skyway, which links downtown Chicago with the Indiana border, for $1.8 billion.

■ Private investors are constructing $7.2 billion of toll roads in Texas under a 50-year lease.

■ The construction of a private toll road recently began near San Diego.

Similar transactions are under consideration. For instance, the governor of New Jersey has proposed a lease of the New Jersey Turnpike and the New York State government is considering leases on the New York State Thruway, Tappan Zee Bridge, and Second Avenue subway.

Historically, with municipal debt financed public infrastructure, such as toll roads, debt-holders receive interest payments guaranteed by the revenue of the toll road. However, they do not directly benefit from a rise in a road's revenue associated with increased traffic or a hike in per-unit tolls. In contrast, investors in the long-term lease of a toll road would be entitled to benefit directly from these factors.

With regard to the performance characteristics of infrastructure, I will focus on toll roads because they seem to be the sub-group with the highest potential activity in the coming years. The actual infrastructure investment vehicle may be a partnership, much like a private equity investment. The behavior of the investment is typically more like fixed-income than equity for two reasons: the stability of revenues, and longer duration (even longer than private equity).

■ In contrast to a private equity investment in a small company, a toll road has monopoly-like characteristics. Its pricing power comes from demand that is not very price-sensitive. Toll road have very high barriers to competition, given limited government funding, little available land, strict environmental regulation, and rising construction costs. It would be very difficult to find a private equity investment in a small company that had a monopoly with strong built-in demand.

■ The duration of an infrastructure investment is much longer term than a private equity investment. As the Chicago Skyway illustrates, some leases have 99-year terms. The investment focus is on a steady growth in revenue rather than an exit strategy (such as selling a private equity company within ten years or so).

While infrastructure is more bond-like than equity-like, it has potentially superior characteristics to traditional bonds:

■ Inflation is a major risk to holders of traditional bonds. In contrast, infrastructure investments have built-in inflation hedges, such as rising traffic and potential toll increases for toll roads. These inflation hedges can make a big difference over time. For example, when it opened in 1951, the New Jersey Turnpike served 787,195 vehicles; fifty years later, it served 230 million vehicles. Tolls increased from $1.50 for the full trip for passenger cars to $6.45. The combined impact drove total revenue from just $18 million in the first full year of operation to $580 million in 2004.

■ Without inflation protection, the valuations of long-duration bonds swing based on interest rate changes. Infrastructure investments not only offer some inflation protection to smooth volatility, they experience very little price volatility in the first place, given that since toll roads are illiquid, their valuation is subjective and infrequent.

Performance is likely to vary by type of infrastructure project. Based on the performance of several new private toll roads around the world, these investments appear to offer returns similar to private equity. However, nearly all of these projects are in their very early stages, in which returns are likely to be equity-like. Once traffic flow on a new toll road becomes established and revenue growth stabilizes, risk dissipates and total returns on the project become more bond-like. It is very early to draw any hard conclusions about performance, but early indications are favorable. As more of these types of deals are undertaken, the market may get a better sense of how they will perform.

Infrastructure may offer excellent diversification to traditional stock and bond investments since the bond-like characteristics result in a low correlation with stocks, and the built-in inflation hedge offers a low correlation with traditional bonds.

While each deal is likely to be unique, infrastructure makes sense as an alternative investment for more conservative investors with a high concentration in traditional bonds and as a substitute for private equity. It also may be valuable for institutions looking for a long-duration asset with low observed volatility, in order to minimize the likelihood of an unexpected mandatory contribution to a pension plan.

Volatility and Hedge Funds

As noted in Chapter 9, rising volatility provides increasing opportunities to benefit from tactical asset allocation. However, another way to capitalize on rising volatility is through exposure to assets that actually benefit from volatility—such as direct investment in stock market volatility and hedge funds.

As mentioned before, volatility and hedge funds differ from other alternative investments because they invest in traditional assets but employ alternative strategies to produce returns. Volatility returns are derived from changes in stock market prices. Hedge funds use strategies such as short sales and arbitrage of stocks and other assets to generate returns that are uncorrelated with the traditional asset classes.

As highlighted in Chapter 5, stock market volatility is cyclical. Exposure to volatility makes sense when it is rising during the second half of the business cycle. Likewise, during the early stage of the business cycle, a short exposure to volatility may be valuable. One measure of volatility is the Chicago Board Options Exchange Volatility Index (VIX for short), which tracks a wide range of S&P 500 options traded on this exchange.

Most traditional asset classes perform poorly as volatility rises. In fact, volatility has a negative correlation, or an inverse relationship, with stock market performance. Just a small allocation to volatility exposure can be valuable in diversifying risk. It is not uncommon for the VIX to rise 50 percent or more as other assets are falling in value. Thus, a small allocation can do a lot.

Some hedge fund styles thrive on volatility because rising volatility can sometimes produce market inefficiencies and mispricings—precisely the situations they seek to exploit through arbitrage opportunities. Although strategies vary, hedge funds are a vehicle for investing in volatility.

During periods when macroeconomic issues (such as oil prices or a presidential election) dominate the market and company-specific fundamentals become a secondary focus, stocks tend to be more highly correlated. In other words, the variation in the performance of individual stocks across the market falls, or becomes tighter. A measurement of the degree of tightness—or the range of performance between the best- and worst-performing stocks in a day—is called "cross-sectional dispersion." When this measurement is low, active managers often find it more difficult to enhance returns through stock picking. In the same way, when cross-sectional dispersion is low, hedge fund managers often find it more difficult to outperform the market using long and short positions.

This is particularly troublesome for market-neutral hedge funds that rely on paired trades to generate returns. The decline in cross-sectional volatility is one explanation for the poor performance of equity hedge fund indexes in 2004. Similarly, convertible-arbitrage hedge fund success depends upon the change in the value of embedded options, which is tied to the outlook for volatility—as volatility rises, so does the value of the embedded option-like exposure.

Hedge fund performance has been highly correlated with volatility, although that relationship weakened somewhat in the late 1990s and early 2000s as the level of volatility itself became more volatile. The instability in the level of volatility has subsided, and I believe that the financial markets have returned to a normal cyclical pattern of implied volatility, which should strengthen the hedge fund/volatility correlation.

Hedge funds are pooled investment vehicles. There is a very wide range of investment strategies employed by different hedge funds throughout the world. Given hedge funds' heterogeneous nature, investors can access a broad spectrum of risk/return parameters through hedge funds, although the funds typically fall into categories with similar characteristics. In order to diversify exposure across hedge fund managers and strategies, investors can invest in a fund of hedge funds that will generally hold anywhere from 10 to 70 individual hedge funds.

Hedge funds are generally sold in private-placement transactions and are often organized as limited partnerships or limited liability companies. In contrast, a mutual fund is a pooled investment vehicle registered with the Securities and Exchange Commission and available to the public. Recently, some hedge funds have registered with the SEC in order to make themselves available to a wider group of investors.

The financial pages of newspapers do not normally include listings for hedge funds. Even in this age of immediate information, there are few (if any) details about specific hedge funds available on the Internet. Why? Because they are private investments for the most part, and many hedge fund managers prefer to keep information about their funds private so as not to attract competitors or copycats.

Today, most hedge funds fall outside much of the regulatory structure and controls imposed by stock exchanges and government regulatory authorities. However, the SEC seems to have a renewed interest in increasing scrutiny. Hedge funds are also free from many of the restrictions imposed on mutual funds, including controls on leverage, short-selling, cross-holding, and derivatives positions.

Many investors cannot answer the question, "What is a hedge fund?" If you are one of them, don't worry. There is a good reason. The term "hedge fund" can be a misnomer. Some hedge funds do not actually hedge against risk. The term applies to a wide range of funds pursuing alternative investment strategies, including funds that may use high-risk strategies without hedging against risk of loss, and funds that pursue lower-risk approaches and hedge market exposure. Although various classification schemes exist, there are four broad types of hedge funds:

- Relative value.
- Event driven.
- Long/short equity.
- Global macro.

Within these categories, a hedge fund can pursue many different strategies that may enhance the portfolio's return. Historically, these specialized investment strategies have provided equity-like returns with various levels of risk. Most importantly, hedge funds have demonstrated performance that is independent of the performance of traditional asset classes. Research also suggests that hedge funds reduce the risk of a diversified portfolio.

Relative Value

Relative-value hedge funds seek to hedge against some type of risk, in one way or another. Their main priority is consistency and stability of return, rather than magnitude of return. Relative-value funds search for relative pricing discrepancies among various securities, related securities, groups of securities, or the overall market. They do not try to determine the direction of the market. As a result, relative-value funds typically have low correlations to the broader equity markets, and may do well in both rising and falling markets. They may generally be able to deliver consistent returns with lower risk of loss, and typically serve to reduce risk in a portfolio. In addition, these funds usually employ leverage to enhance returns.

There are three major subcategories of relative value hedge funds: convertible arbitrage, market-neutral, and fixed-income arbitrage.

Convertible Arbitrage

Convertible-arbitrage hedge funds use one of the more conservative hedge fund investing strategies. Convertible-arb funds invest in convertible securities, usually preferred shares or bonds, and hedge the exposure by selling short the underlying common stock. The key to their success is being able to take advantage of mispricings between the corresponding securities. Because managers typically take long positions in convertible bonds, the strategy typically does not perform well during environments of rising interest rates or widening credit spreads, although many managers attempt to hedge some of these risks to varying degrees. When the underlying equity's volatility rises, the strategy tends to do well, with the inverse occurring during drops in volatility.

Market Neutral

Market-neutral hedge funds use a strategy that involves having equally long and short equities. In theory, being dollar, beta, and sector neutral greatly reduces market risk. Managers using this strategy seek returns that are independent of general market movements. The managers' ability to select individual securities (both on the long and short sides) drives most of the fund's performance, as opposed to the direction of the equity markets. Security selection techniques often include both fundamental and quantitative factors.

Fixed-Income Arbitrage

Fixed-income-arbitrage hedge funds seek to profit by exploiting mispricings between fixed-income securities, while using leverage to boost returns. Generally, a fund will take a long and a short position in two securities, hoping to capture the deviation in pricing. In addition, most managers will hedge interest rate risk. Typical trades include yield curve, credit spread, and cash/futures arbitrage. Because returns from each trade are usually low, fixed-income-arbitrage managers tend to use higher leverage than the other strategies.

Event Driven

Event-driven hedge funds use strategies that depend on an event, such as a merger/acquisition, spin-off, bankruptcy reorganization, or recapitalization, as the catalyst to release intrinsic value. These strategies typically rely heavily on fundamental research, rather than quantitative models. Some event-driven managers shift between the risk-arbitrage and distressed-securities strategies (see below). Given their higher correlation to traditional stock and bond asset classes, these strategies generally enhance portfolio returns while providing some diversification benefits.

There are two major subcategories of event-driven hedge funds: risk arbitrage and distressed securities.

Risk (Merger) Arbitrage

Risk-arbitrage hedge funds use a strategy that typically involves the simultaneous purchase of stock in a company being acquired and the sale of stock of its acquirer. While the acquisition or merger is pending, the stock of the company being acquired will generally trade at a discount to the per-share price being offered by the acquiring company.

This pricing disparity reflects uncertainty about the outcome of the merger. If the takeover plan falls through, the stock price of the targeted company may decline. Many risk-arbitrage funds reduce risk by trading only in friendly takeovers after they are announced (as opposed to speculating on hostile takeovers even before an official public offer has been made). Risk-arbitrage managers often use equity options as a low-risk alternative to the outright purchase or sale of common stock. The key risks to this strategy are a slowdown in merger/acquisition activity and a hostile regulatory environment.

Distressed Securities

Distressed-securities hedge funds use a strategy that focuses on the securities of companies in bankruptcy and reorganization. These funds purchase various types of securities, from senior debt (low risk) to common stock (high risk) of distressed companies. Investments tend to be longer term in nature due to the length of restructurings. Negative events and the subsequent announcement of a proposed restructuring or reorganization often create a severe market imbalance, because some holders of the company's securities attempt to sell their positions at a time when few investors are willing to buy. The strategy is successful if the distressed company emerges from difficulty and its securities appreciate. Favorable returns typically occur after recessionary periods, when equities are performing well and credit spreads narrow.

Long/Short Equity

The third category of hedge fund strategies is "long/short equity," which represents the largest category of hedge fund assets as a percentage of total hedge fund assets. This type of fund is dependent on the direction of markets. Managers hedge some market risk through short positions that seek to provide profits in a market downturn in order to offset losses created by the long positions. In some cases, managers hold only short positions, which generally perform very well in down markets.

Managers will use varying degrees of leverage and net exposure (gross longs minus gross shorts) to the equity markets, and can focus on specific geographic regions or industry sectors. Except for pure short sellers, these strategies usually have relatively higher levels of correlation with equity markets, and typically act to increase portfolio returns while providing protection during down markets.

Long/short hedge funds generally fall into four subcategories: U.S. long/short, global/international long/short, sector-based, and short only.

U.S. Long/Short

The U.S. long/short is the strategy most often referred to as the *typical* hedge fund and it is used by the majority of managers today. This bottom-up approach involves selecting individual equities to purchase or sell short in an effort to reduce broad market exposure and to profit as the purchased securities appreciate and those sold short decline. Managers in this style generally increase net-long equity exposure in bull markets and decrease net-long exposure in bear markets.

Global/International Long-Short

Global/international long/short involves investing outside the United States, using both long- and short-equity exposure. In addition, some managers focus exclusively on the equity and fixed-income markets of emerging markets, usually maintaining long-only positions due to limited shorting opportunities.

Sector Based

Sector-based funds focus on a manager's particular area of investment expertise, such as technology, financials, energy, and health care.

Short Selling

Short sellers sell a security that they do not own (they actually borrow it from someone else) with the expectation of buying it at a lower price than the price at which they sold it (when it is time to return it to the lender). This strategy seeks to profit from an expected decline in the price of the security. Short selling has a negative correlation with equities—it performs extremely well during down markets, but lags significantly in bull markets.

Global Macro (Tactical Trading)

Some of the most well-known managers belong to a hedge fund category called global macro. These funds seek to benefit from trends or market moves in equity, fixed-income, currency, or commodity markets. The returns can be high, but so can the losses because the leveraged directional investments (which are not hedged) tend to have the largest impact on fund performance. Overall, they tend to have low correlation with traditional asset classes, while providing the potential for attractive returns and higher volatility. The dispersion of returns among managers is significant due to their high levels of investment flexibility.

There are two major subcategories of global-macro, tactical-trading hedge funds: discretionary and systematic.

Discretionary

Discretionary managers tend to make concentrated bets based on fundamental and technical analysis. These are known as "top-down" strategies because they concentrate on exploiting perceived price divergences between asset classes, rather than the securities-specific companies. The funds typically take long and short positions in currencies, bonds, equities, and commodities.

Some countries, notably the United Kingdom and Malaysia, have blamed specific global-macro hedge funds for profiting from the efforts of central banks to prop up their currencies. In the United Kingdom, the result was its forced exit from the Exchange Rate Mechanism in 1992. For Malaysia, it was one of the factors that led to the imposition of capital controls in 1998. Although an easy target for blame, there is conflicting evidence as to whether hedge funds were the cause of such occurrences.

Systematic

Systematic managers invest based on quantitative models that tend to follow trends. They often hold multiple positions in many markets. Most systematic hedge funds are designated as managed-futures funds —taking long and short positions in liquid financial futures, such as commodities, currencies, interest rates, and stock market indexes.

Hedge Fund Performance Characteristics

In general, hedge funds use trading strategies that generate performance that is generally independent of the direction of the capital markets. Hedge funds typically have a low correlation to traditional asset classes. The performance of the average hedge fund, as measured by the fund of funds index, has a low 0.43 correlation with the stock market, and 0.10 with the bond market. In short, hedge fund strategies are excellent diversifiers of equity market exposure, and a diversified portfolio of hedge funds may produce more-predictable returns than the stock market. Hedge funds also are largely independent of the movement of fixed-income securities.

To demonstrate the benefits of an allocation to hedge funds in a portfolio of traditional assets, we can examine the portfolio's historical performance during down periods in the equity market. Since 1990, only during three months, when the S&P 500 declined, did the fund of hedge funds index underperform the stock market. The worst monthly return for the S&P 500 was −14.5 percent in August 1998, whereas the fund of funds index fell only 7.5 percent during that month. In fact, this was the worst-performing month for the fund of funds index since 1990. In September 2002, the S&P 500 fell 10.9 percent, far more than the fund of funds index, which fell only 0.5 percent. In more than half of the months that the market declined during the 1990–2003 period, the fund of hedge funds index posted a gain. However, an allocation to hedge funds represented by several different hedge fund strategies may lag in up-equity markets. In December 1991, the S&P 500 turned in its best one-month return for the period—11.4 percent—while the fund of funds benchmark returned 4.5 percent for that month.

As I mentioned before, hedge fund performance has been highly correlated with volatility, although that relationship weakened somewhat in the late 1990s and early 2000s as the level of volatility became more volatile. The instability in the level of volatility has subsided as we have returned to a normal cyclical pattern of implied volatility, which should strengthen the hedge fund/volatility correlation. I expect an average return of 5–7 percent for a moderate volatility hedge fund.

It is important to remember to assess risk qualitatively, as well as quantitatively, when it comes to alternative investments. Many hedge funds suffered a disastrous 1998, when Russia defaulted on its debt in

August. The repercussions of this crisis spread to other countries and caused a panic among many investors, causing deviations from normal market relationships. Investors fled to quality debt instruments, reversing the trend in credit spreads. The resulting massive sell-offs caused an increase in the liquidity-risk premium for non-government bonds in the United States. Hedge funds that used leverage in anticipation of narrowing spreads suffered dramatic losses, and were forced to liquidate their portfolios under margin calls from lenders. The credit squeeze on hedge funds, together with investor withdrawals, led to losses for most funds, specifically the relative-value and global-macro funds that rely heavily on leverage. In one case, the plight of the hedge fund Long-Term Capital Management was so extreme that it prompted the Federal Reserve to restructure the claims of the lenders to avoid a forced liquidation that could have resulted in a collapse of the international debt markets.

Finally, while changes to the tax code in recent years have reduced the impact of taxes on investment strategies, hedge funds are not very tax-efficient. Successful managers generate absolute return more through risk control (being long when the asset is going up, and neutral or short when it is going down) than by timing entry and exit points correctly. Managers often reduce positions dynamically as they are losing money, and increase them dynamically as they are making money. The level of trading activity aligns directly to the volatility of the market. As a result, hedge fund turnover can be high. Most hedge fund gains fall into the short-term category for tax purposes.

A balanced asset allocation can achieve a 3 percent allocation to volatility and hedge funds (within a range of 0 to 10 percent) through volatility exposure that uses futures or swaps, or through a mix of hedge funds of varying styles. For investors with the ability to allocate to illiquid alternative investments with favorable characteristics, their allocation to volatility is less. You can think of volatility and hedge funds as an alternative to the other alternatives. In other words, you may want to reduce your exposure to volatility when opportunities to fund superior private equity or real estate investments arise, and increase your exposure to volatility if superior alternatives are not available.

By introducing an allocation to hedge funds in a portfolio otherwise composed of traditional asset classes, investors can benefit in the following ways:

■ Historically low correlation with a portfolio consisting of traditional asset classes can potentially improve the portfolio's risk/return profile, while providing capital preservation during poor equity markets and upside participation during positive equity markets.

■ Attractive risk-adjusted returns, as measured by hedge fund strategy indexes, have been generated in the past, even after accounting for survivorship bias and taxes.

Investors who are more aggressive may benefit from investing a larger portion of total assets in a fund of hedge funds given my recommended 30 percent allocation to alternative investments. The competitive returns, large degree of independence from the direction of the equity market (where most of the aggressive portfolio assets are), and moderate standard deviation generally favor a slightly higher allocation to volatility and hedge funds to potentially enhance return and diversify risk of a more aggressive portfolio.

Similarly, conservative portfolios may benefit from hedge funds' low correlation with the bond market as well as the stock market. Volatility exposure may not be as much of a benefit to a conservative portfolio that has less need for a hedge against stock market losses (given its lower exposure to stocks). However, hedge funds, which have a volatility only slightly higher than the bond market over the 1990–2005 period, can help even an investor with lower risk tolerances attain their portfolio objectives. An allocation of around 3 percent to hedge funds may benefit a more conservative or income-oriented portfolio.

CHAPTER 12

The New Style Is Cyclicality

This chapter predicts an evolution in the way the markets define asset-class style: from growth and value, to defensive (high quality) and cyclical (low quality).

When defined by valuation, style reflects sensitivity to the business cycle. Value has been more cyclical and growth less cyclical (or defensive).

- The composition and characteristics of growth and value underwent an evolution in the late 1990s, as the information technology sector (a very cyclical sector) grew to dominate the growth index, changing the historical pattern of style performance.
- Style defined by growth and value is less likely to provide as much of a difference in performance, since relative cyclicality of growth and value is not as different as in the past and therefore not as valuable in defining asset classes in the future.
- Defining style as cyclical and defensive rather than growth and value continues the legacy of style diversification and tactical risk management in the new era of investment performance.

Style Cyclicality

As presented in Chapter 7, the style classifications of growth and value have existed since the early 1970s. Today, professional investors use them to benchmark billions in equity investments. Standard and Poor's and Frank Russell Company produce the most widely used growth and value indexes. Both providers have some indexes with track records back to the 1970s.

Since their inception, the price-to-book ratio has been the primary factor that defines growth and value for both the S&P and Russell style indexes. Stocks with high price-to-book ratios have made up the growth indexes, and stocks with low price-to-book ratios populate the value indexes.

The price-to-book ratio is simply a stock's price per share divided by its book value per share. To calculate book value per share, divide a company's book value (assets minus liabilities) by the number of shares of stock outstanding. In theory, it represents the value a shareholder would receive if the company were liquidated. Why not use the price-to-earnings ratio? A stock's P/E ratio can vary widely during the earnings cycle, especially for cyclical companies. The price-to-book ratio is much more consistent. In general, companies with very cyclical earnings patterns have consistently low price-to-book ratios and companies that are more stable growers have consistently high price-to-book ratios. The price-to-book ratio does not measure earnings volatility, but it does reflect the market's assessment of the relative cyclicality of a company. Therefore, price-to-book was a good proxy for style.

In the past, the performance of growth and value indexes were tied to the business cycle. The steadier growth of high price-to-book stocks fared better during recessions. For this reason, growth stocks are often called defensive. Value stocks have a more volatile earnings pattern given their heightened sensitivity to the business cycle. Therefore, value stocks are considered cyclical.

The sector weightings within the two styles are an easy way to see their differences in cyclicality. Historically, a large concentration of stocks with relatively high price-to-book ratios were in the healthcare and consumer staples sectors. The demand for healthcare and basic household products is relatively unaffected by the business cycle. Therefore, these defensive sectors made up a large portion of the growth indexes. Sectors with traditionally low price-to-book ratios include materials and energy. The demand for commodities is tied to the business cycle. Therefore, these sectors fall almost exclusively into the value indexes.

Style Evolution

In recent years, the sector composition of the growth and value styles has evolved away from cyclicality. This has led to relative style performance that is out of sync with traditional relationship to the business cycle.

The composition and characteristics of growth and value underwent an evolution in the late 1990s. At the start of the 1990s, the information technology sector (a group of cyclical companies) made up more than 10 percent of the S&P 500 Value Index but only about 5 percent of the S&P 500 Growth Index. However, as the technology sector grew during the 1990s, it increased to more than 50 percent of the Growth Index by the end of the decade. Investors believed the tech sector had become immune to swings in the business cycle. At the same time, the telecommunications services sector (a defensive group of companies) fell from 14 percent of the Growth Index in 1990 to just 4 percent by 2000, as deregulation sharply increased the earnings volatility of these companies. Shifts in the Value Index mirrored these shifts in the Growth Index. The changes in the constituents of the indexes produced an evolution in the pattern of style performance.

Despite what investors believed at the end of the 1990s, we know now that the information technology sector is still very cyclical. Nevertheless, info tech still dominates the Growth Index. While its weighting has fallen from the highs of 2000, the tech sector comprises 25 percent of the Growth Index, or five times its weighting at the start of the 1990s. The information technology sector's new dominance of the growth style resulted in a reversal of the traditional cyclical pattern of relative style performance. The historically defensive Growth Index underperformed the Value Index during the recession and related bear market of the early 2000s. It is unlikely that the traditional cyclical pattern of performance has returned after the aberrant period of the late 1990s and early 2000s.

The mixing of cyclical and defensive sectors in both indexes has muted the relative cyclicality of growth and value. This leads to the question, "What will the pattern and magnitude of future style cycles be?" It is highly likely that a new pattern of relative performance will exist for the growth and value styles. The relative cyclicality of growth and value will not be as divergent as in the past. Style will fail to provide as much of a difference in relative performance as it had in the past. Therefore, style may not be as valuable in defining asset classes for the purposes of diversification or tactical risk management.

The S&P Earnings and Dividend rankings, also known as quality ratings, are an effective tool for illustrating this unfavorable shift in style dynamics. This measurement of the relative cyclicality of earnings and dividends illustrates the traditional performance relationship between cyclical and defensive stocks, and how the performance of growth and value indexes have differed recently due to their compositional changes.

> The S&P Earnings and Dividend Rankings measure the relative cyclicality of earnings and dividends. Stocks have grades from A through D. A+ is the highest quality ranking; it reflects consistency and a low degree of cyclicality. D is the lowest rating; it indicates that the company is in bankruptcy. C is the lowest rating for a company not in bankruptcy or liquidation, and reflects poor consistency in earnings and dividends generally associated with a high degree of cyclicality.

In the S&P 500, a predominantly high-quality index on this measure, about 50 percent of companies have an A (A+ through A-) rating and a little over 40 percent have a B (B+ through B-) rating. Only a few have a rating of C or are not rated at all. A company does not have a rating if it has a track record as a public company of less than five years. To compare the S&P Growth and Value Indexes to S&P 500 quality ratings, we will call the A-rated companies "high quality" and B-rated companies "low quality."

High Quality=A=Defensive=old Growth
Low Quality=B=Cyclical=old Value

A very tight relationship between the relative performance of high- and low-quality stocks and growth and value stocks existed until the late 1990s. The relative performance of high-quality and low-quality stocks in the S&P 500 followed the typical cyclical pattern of performance. Low-quality, cyclical stocks began to outperform in 1998–1999, as the business cycle overheated. Then, high-quality, defensive stocks outperformed, as the recession took place. A return to lower quality outperformance during the recovery followed. This pattern mirrored what happened in the late 1980s, when the economy was overheating and the relative performance of low-quality stocks improved—that is until the recession in 1990, when high-quality stocks outperformed. As the recovery ensued, low-quality stock outperformance followed in the early 1990s. See Figure 12.1.

In summary, the pattern of growth and value tracked that of high-quality and low-quality stocks tightly until 1998, when changes in the constituents of the indexes resulted in the erratic style behavior of the late 1990s. The traditionally defensive growth stocks surged as the economy went into overdrive, then plunged to record relative underperformance as the business cycle fell into recession and then finally re-coupled with the traditional cyclical pattern measured by the quality indexes as the information technology sector weight moderated in the growth index.

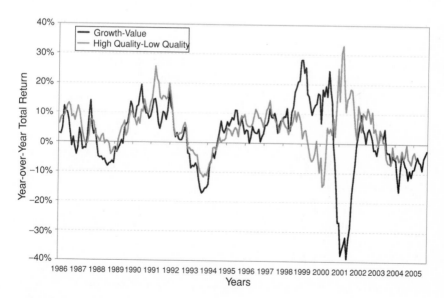

FIGURE 12.1   Relative performance by style.
Year-over-year total return of S&P 500 Growth less Value and S&P 500 A-rated stocks less B-rated.

Conflicts In Cyclicality and Valuation

It appears from the chart that the traditional relationship between cyclicality and style performance has re-emerged. However, I cannot be so sure. There is a lingering shift in the growth and value composition, which the current sector weightings reflect.

- The information technology sector has by far the largest weighting among the low-quality, cyclical stocks at 24 percent. However, it only makes up 7 percent of the cyclical Value Index. The sector's representation is much larger in the historically defensive growth index at 24 percent.
- The financials sector makes up the largest weight among the high-quality, defensive stocks at 30 percent. However, it represents only 3 percent of the historically defensive Growth Index. The sector now makes up 36 percent of the historically cyclical Value Index.

Since the top-weighted sectors in the cyclical and style measures are in conflict, it may be unlikely that the tight relationship between them that existed prior to 1998 will re-emerge permanently. I believe that the performance of cyclicality (measured by the quality ratings) and style (defined by growth and value) will diverge in the future, as the business cycle unfolds. The evolution of style may require a new asset class definition.

Why are financials considered a high-quality, defensive sector? The financial sector has achieved stable margins and earnings growth due to many factors.

- Changes in regulations led to better diversity in lending and funding, and enabled companies to achieve greater efficiencies through consolidation.
- Technology also drove efficiency improvements.
- Diversification into new transaction-based lines of business reduced dependence on interest-rate-generated income.
- Companies faced a more stable interest rate environment, compared to the 1970s and 1980s.

- Strategies to match the duration of their assets and liabilities improved.
- New tools to manage and diversify credit exposure were used.

The financial sector proved to be more diversified and defensive in nature during the 2001 recession. In contrast to prior downturns, no major earnings repercussions stemmed from the largest corporate and sovereign credit defaults in history.

Why is information technology considered cyclical and low quality? The business cycle still drives the demand for technology products and services. As businesses seek to grow profits, they spend on new technology. As profits slip, companies defer technology spending until the recovery. Furthermore, the intense competition and relentless introduction of new technologies, as well as shorter product life cycles that destabilize the earnings pattern and result in volatile profit margins and earnings further complicate the cyclicality of the IT sector.

Adapting Style

In order to benefit from the diversification and tactical opportunities historically associated with cyclical and defensive stocks, adaptation may be necessary in view of the evolution in composition and characteristics of the market. The Growth and Value Indexes are unlikely to vary in performance as widely as they did in the past. In addition, the business cycle dynamics of relative growth and value performance have become ambiguous, rendering less effective our tactical tools for forecasting relative performance and managing risk.

As mentioned before, when growth was in favor it historically outperformed value (and vice-versa) by an annualized average of 8 percent. I expect less of a performance difference between growth and value over the next ten years. Several factors support the outlook for muted relative performance:

- Style composition is now more evenly distributed across cyclical and defensive industries than in the 1970s or 1980s, when growth was dominated by the defensive consumer staples and health care sectors.

■ Although the value style has a slightly higher proportion of lower-quality companies, the quality breakdown is more evenly distributed than in the past. See Figure 12.2.

■ The characteristics of growth and value have converged somewhat and, in recent years, the difference in valuation, dividend yield, and median company size has narrowed significantly from the long-term average.

The Growth and Value Indexes have demonstrated increasing sector concentration. One sector rose sharply in the 1990s to dominate each index. Information technology rose to more than 50 percent of the Growth Index at its peak, and one-third of the Value Index is concentrated in financials. This has resulted in more company-specific and industry-specific factors driving relative style performance in recent years. The greater sector diversification of stocks grouped into cyclical and

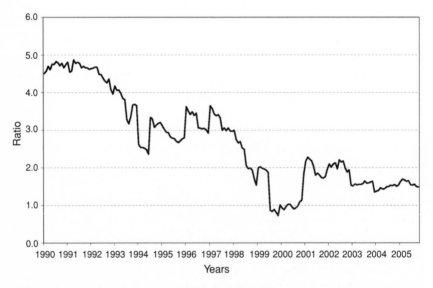

FIGURE 12.2   Low quality stocks in Growth Index relative to low quality stocks in
             Value Index.
Ratio of B-rated stocks relative to A-rated stocks in S&P 500 style indexes.

defensive categories, or low- and high-quality categories, should help to keep relative performance driven by top-down, economic factors. The evolution of growth and value necessitates the adaptation of style in order to continue the effectiveness of tactical risk management tools.

In contrast to the muted relative performance outlook for growth and value, I expect the same magnitude of relative performance between cyclical and defensive stocks as in the past. Defining style by cyclical and defensive traits, rather than by growth and value, continues the legacy of style diversification and tactical risk management in the new era of investment performance.

Then, why not recommend cyclical and defensive instead of growth and value as the style part of the strategic asset allocation framework presented in Part 2? Because it is easier said than done. Unfortunately, there are no independently produced cyclical (low-quality) and defensive (high-quality) indexes that are compatible and include the entire stock market. In the next few years, as the industry catches up with this idea, I believe that there will be widely available indexes, exchange-traded funds, and mutual funds for use in allocating on the basis of cyclicality.

Until then, you may achieve a cyclical-style approach through assembling a market-capitalization weighted portfolio of A-rated and B-rated stocks, and tactically allocating between them. However, doing so would require shifts among a large number of individual stock holdings, which may be costly and time consuming, and may entail extensive research at the company-specific level.

Style Methodology Change

S&P changed their methodology for constructing their Growth and Value Indexes at the end of 2005. After decades of solely using price-to-book ratio to determine style, they adopted a number of other measures, including earnings growth rates and other valuation measures. However, these measures are highly correlated with the price-to-book ratio and do not measure cyclicality directly, as do the S&P Earnings and Dividend rankings. The changes to the S&P style index methodology are unlikely to restore the former relationship between growth and value, and defensive and cyclical performance.

Fortunately, until the next major shift in the business cycle (say 3–6 years from now), there may not be a dramatic difference in the performance of the traditional growth and value style asset class distinction and cyclical-style approach—indeed, they have performed together for four years now. Hopefully, by the next shift, the markets will have adapted to the concept and introduced indexes and investment products based on the new style of cyclicality, or quality.

CHAPTER 13

Active and Passive Investing

Throughout this book, I have approached investing from the top down by defining and allocating to asset classes, rather than from the bottom up by assembling a portfolio security-by-security. Now that you have the tools to construct your asset allocation, it is time to focus on how to achieve your desired exposures to asset classes. In other words, this chapter answers the question, "How do you implement the strategies presented in this book?"

There are two approaches you can take when looking at investment vehicles from the top down: passive investment management and active investment management.

- Indexing, or passive management, involves investing in individual securities with the intention of replicating a market index. In other words, a passively managed mutual fund or Exchange Traded Fund (ETF) attempts to mimic the performance of an index as closely as possible. Most of these investment vehicles have been successful in tightly tracking whichever index they follow.
- Alternatively, active management involves investing in individual securities, with the intention of outperforming the index. For bonds and large-cap stocks, actively managed mutual funds failed, on average, to outperform their respective indexes in the 1980s, 1990s, and so far in the 2000s.

Index-tracking ETFs and mutual funds represent the purest implementation of the strategies outlined in this book. It would seem that a
passive approach to each asset class would be most suitable. But should
you rule out active investing entirely in the new era of investment performance? To answer this question, several points are worth reviewing.

- In theory, the characteristics of assets classes indicate which
  approach is superior.
- In practice, the past performance of active managers in each major
  asset class indicates which approach has yielded superior results.
- A blend of passive and active management may offer the best of
  both worlds.

Characteristics of Inefficient Markets

For more than forty years, academics have debated whether financial
markets are efficient. In theory, a market is efficient if securities prices
fully reflect all current, relevant information—not only what has happened in the past, but what market participants expect to happen in the
future. If a market is efficient, then the current market price of a security is a good estimate of its intrinsic value. If that is true, then no analysis or information gives one investor an advantage over another.
Consequently, active portfolio managers are unlikely to outperform
their benchmark consistently in efficient markets.

In the United States, capital markets are well developed—investors
have good access to information and the ability to act on that information almost instantaneously. The debatable question is whether markets
are perfectly efficient or just somewhat efficient. In less-than-perfectly-
efficient asset classes, managers have demonstrated some ability to
outperform their benchmark. Those asset classes share the following
characteristics:

- Information that is not readily available or requires superior expertise to analyze. In some cases, new information does not dissemi-
  nate instantaneously to all investors. (You should not confuse
  having superior access to information with having access to inside
  information. It is illegal to trade on inside information.) In other

cases, unique expertise is required to analyze new information quickly. An active manager with better access to information and/or specific knowledge to decipher it may have an advantage over other investors.

■ Fewer analysts covering securities. In general, the greater the number of analysts covering a security, the more rapidly information is disseminated. In theory, this should lead to more efficient pricing of securities. Alternatively, if the analyst coverage within an asset class is thin, the class tends to be less efficient. Large-cap stocks have extensive analyst coverage, generally ranging from four to thirty-five analysts per stock (see Table 13.1). Small-cap stocks tend to have significantly fewer analysts assigned to them, generally ranging from zero to nineteen (see Table 13.2).

■ Low levels of liquidity. Stocks or bonds that do not trade on a regular basis or that trade only a small percentage of shares outstanding are illiquid. These securities may offer active investors the opportunity to take advantage of pricing inefficiencies. Those asset classes that have a greater number of illiquid securities may be less efficient.

■ High transaction costs. Low liquidity can inhibit investors' ability to purchase or sell a security in a timely manner without adversely

TABLE 13.1   Deep Analyst Coverage among Large Cap Stocks
Range of Number of Analysts Covering Largest and Smallest Stocks in S&P 500

Largest S&P 500 Stocks	Analyst Coverage	Smallest S&P 500 Stocks	Analyst Coverage
Exxon Mobil	23	Big Lots Inc.	8
General Electric	24	PMC-Sierra	16
Microsoft	36	Maytag	6
Citigroup	23	Hercules	4
Procter & Gamble	26	Calpine	15
Johnson & Johnson	20	Dana	15
Bank of America	33	Visteon	11
American International Group	23	Gateway	12
Pfizer	35	Cooper Tire & Rubber	6
Altria Group	15	Applied Micro Circuits Corp.	12

TABLE 13.2   Relatively Thin Analyst Coverage among Small Cap Stocks
Range of Number of Analysts Covering Largest and Smallest Stocks in S&P 500

Largest S&P 500 Stocks	Analyst Coverage	Smallest S&P 500 Stocks	Analyst Coverage
Southwestern Energy	11	Cryolife Inc.	2
NVR Inc	5	ESS Technology	7
Roper Industries	13	Rewards Network Inc.	2
The Cooper Cos. Inc.	10	Theragenics Corp.	0
Oshkosh Truck Corp.	9	Wolverine Tube Inc.	1
Cimarex Energy	9	Magnetec Inc.	3
Massey Energy	11	Zix Corp.	1
Pharmaceutical Product Dev. Inc.	11	Fedders Corp.	1
Global Payments Inc.	19	Osteotech Inc.	0
Vintage Petroleum Inc.	14	Meade Instruments Corp.	0

affecting its price. An investor may chose to break up a large trade into smaller pieces to have less market impact, which can result in higher transaction costs.

Small-cap and international stocks tend to have the above characteristics. These lesser-efficient asset classes may be better suited to active management. Bonds and large-cap U.S. stocks tend not to share these characteristics, and thus may be more efficient. You could, at least in part, use a passive indexed approach to investment selection in these asset classes.

Analysis of Asset Class Efficiency

An effective way to measure the degree of efficiency of an asset class is to examine what percentage of actively managed mutual funds outperformed the respective index for the asset class. To do so, I analyzed the performance of thousands of active portfolio managers across different asset classes in the Lipper (a Reuters company) mutual fund database. The results? Only in the bond and large-cap U.S. stock asset classes did the average active manager underperform the benchmark (during the measurement period for that class, determined by availability of data). Active managers in other asset classes outperformed their appropriate benchmark, on average.

■ Large-cap core U.S. equity: Only 43 percent of actively managed mutual funds in this class beat the S&P 500 on average, for rolling 12-month periods during the past 30 years. Breaking the results down by style, 48 percent of actively managed large-cap growth funds outperformed their respective index, and 40 percent of actively managed large-cap value funds outperformed their index. See Figure 13.1.

■ Small-cap U.S. equity: A total of 53 percent of actively managed small-cap mutual funds beat the S&P SmallCap 600 Index, on average, for rolling 12-month periods during the past 19 years.

■ International equity: A full 57 percent of actively managed international mutual funds beat the Morgan Stanley Capital International Europe, Australia, and the Far East (MSCI EAFE) Index on average for rolling 12-month periods during the past 15 years.

■ U.S. Bonds: Only 29 percent of actively managed bond mutual funds benchmarked to the Lehman Brothers U.S. Aggregate Bond Index outperformed, on average, for rolling 12-month periods during the past 20 years. Municipal bond fund managers fared similarly, with only 30 percent of active managers outperforming the Lehman Brothers Municipal Bond Index over the past 20 years.

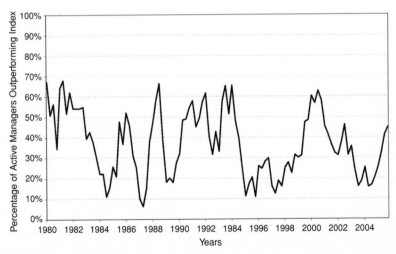

FIGURE 13.1   Less than half of actively managed large-cap funds outperform the Index.

Percentage of large-cap core active managers in the Lipper database outperforming the S&P 500 over the prior four quarters.

Source: Lipper, a Reuters Company.

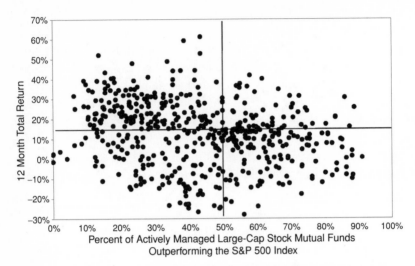

FIGURE 13.2   Relative performance of actively managed large-cap stock funds.
S&P 500 Index performance for 12 month rolling periods for 30 years ending 2005
and percent of actively managed large-cap stock funds outperforming the Index.
Source: Lipper, a Reuters Company.

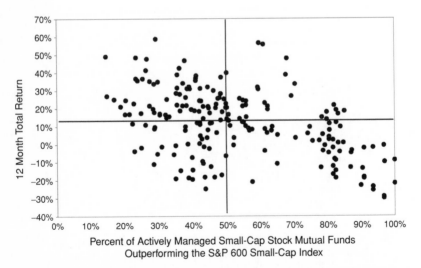

FIGURE 13.3   Relative performance of actively managed small-cap stock funds.
S&P 600 Small-Cap Index performance for 12 month rolling periods for 19 years
ending 2005 and percent of actively managed small-cap stock funds outperforming
the Index.
Source: Lipper, a Reuters Company.

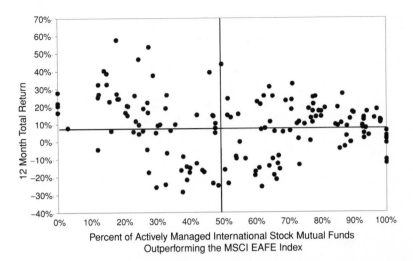

FIGURE 13.4 Relative performance of actively managed international stock funds. MSCI EAFE Index performance for 12 month rolling periods for 15 years ending 2005 and percent of actively managed international stock funds outperforming the Index. Source: Lipper, a Reuters Company.

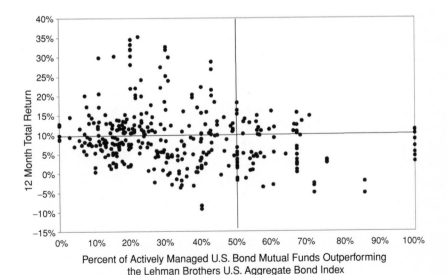

FIGURE 13.5 Relative performance of actively managed bond funds. Lehman Aggregate Bond Index performance for 12 month rolling periods for 20 years ending 2005 and percent of actively managed bond funds outperforming the Index. Source: Lipper, a Reuters Company.

What do the Dots mean?

Active managers tend to perform better than their respective index when returns are below average. In these charts, each dot represents a 12-month rolling time period for the average of all fund managers—during the past 30 years for large-cap, 19 years for small-cap, 15 years for international, and 20 years for U.S. bonds. The horizontal line dissecting the graph represents the average return of all active managers in that style over the period measured.

Notice that more of the dots fall in the top left and lower right quadrants of the charts. This indicates that active managers have been more likely to underperform the index when index returns are above their long-term average, and perform better on a relative basis when returns for the index are below their long-term average. Further research reveals that this pattern is the result of active managers having, on average, slightly less volatility than their benchmark index.

Interestingly, the average large-cap U.S. core mutual fund manager has underperformed the S&P 500 by an average of 0.5 percentage points per year during the past 30 years. In contrast, small-cap U.S. stock and international stock fund managers generally have been able to beat their indexes over time. Will these two asset classes continue to outperform in the future? Maybe in the short run. However, given their shorter track record (15 to 19 years vs. 30 years) and the cyclicality of relative performance, I think that U.S. small-cap and international stocks may eventually become more efficient, although such a trend is not yet observable.

Market characteristics have an impact on active manager relative performance. Large-cap stocks in the S&P 500 benefit from rapid information dissemination, are widely covered by analysts, are liquid, and generally trade efficiently with regard to transaction costs. In short, active managers in this asset class are less likely to outperform on a consistent basis. In the small-cap U.S. asset class, the market's large number of securities, limited research coverage, and low trading volume can result in inefficiencies. These inefficiencies increase active managers' potential to add value over the index. Similarly, within the international stock market, different levels of research coverage and liquidity can promote inefficiencies that benefit active managers.

About the data:

Small-cap and international funds have a shorter track record than large-cap funds—our analysis period for those asset classes began with the first month having at least 20 funds in the database, or 19 years for small cap and 15 for international. Furthermore, the entire Lipper mutual fund database is subject to certain limitations, including:

- Survivorship bias: Funds that were closed or merged into other funds are excluded from the databases.
- Potential classification errors: Funds are assumed to have always been part of the asset class that currently defines them, even though it is possible that they could previously have been benchmarked to another asset class.
- Multiple fund classes: Classes of funds derived from the same original portfolio but having different fee structures are included.

You can make adjustments to minimize the impact of some of these factors, but not all of them. Modifying the data set several different ways to adjust for the limitations reveals no material difference in the outcome.

The data reveals several additional insights about the dynamics of active manager performance.

- Active managers performed worse, relative to their benchmark, when their asset class was in favor with investors compared to when their asset class was out of favor. This finding held across all asset classes.
- On average, active managers displayed less volatility than their respective indexes. This finding also held across all asset classes.
- The degree to which an active manager's performance tended to vary from that of the index (known as tracking error) had an impact on relative performance. Managers with performance that closely tracked their benchmark index (low tracking error) tended to have poorer relative performance than those with performance that strayed from the index's performance (high tracking error).

What do the Dots mean this time?

In Figures 13.6 to 13.9, each dot represents the relative performance of an active manager versus the index over the entire historical period—during the past 30 years for large-cap, 19 years for small-cap and 15 years for international—along with the standard deviation of that relative performance, which represents tracking error. The plot of dots in each chart slopes upward. This suggests that higher tracking error across asset classes coincides with better relative performance in each asset class.

Active and Passive: The Best of Both Worlds

Based on theoretical and practical evidence, the efficiency of U.S. large-cap stocks and U.S. bonds makes it worth considering a passive approach—using exchange-traded funds or index-tracking mutual funds for these asset classes. The same evidence reveals the relative

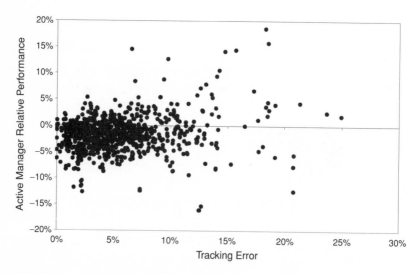

FIGURE 13.6   Active large-cap managers with higher tracking error have offered better relative performance.

Active large-cap managers relative performance and tracking error for 30 years ending 2005

Source: Lipper, a Reuters Company.

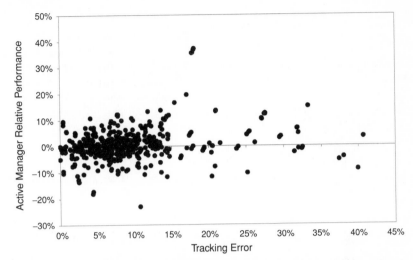

FIGURE 13.7   Active small-cap managers with higher tracking error have offered better relative performance.
Active small-cap managers relative performance and tracking error to S&P 600 Index for 19 years ending 2005.
Source: Lipper, a Reuters Company.

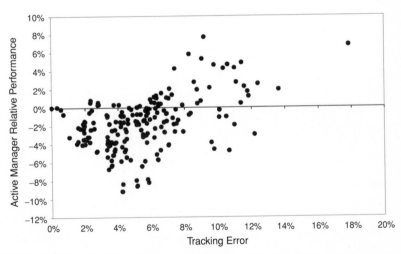

FIGURE 13.8   Active international managers with higher tracking error have offered better relative performance.
Active international managers relative performance and tracking error to MSCI EAFE index for 15 years ending 2005.
Source: Lipper, a Reuters Company.

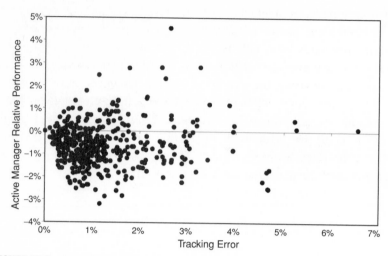

FIGURE 13.9   Active bond managers with higher tracking error have offered better
relative performance.
Active bond managers relative performance and tracking error to Lehman Aggregate Bond Index for twenty years.
Source: Lipper, a Reuters Company.

inefficiency of the other major asset classes, and suggests actively managed investment vehicles may offer superior results to an index.

Should all bonds and large-cap stock investments be passive? Given
the historical evidence, it would be easy to answer "Yes." But in the
future … maybe not. Some active management of these asset classes
may prove to be valuable in the new era of investment performance.
To see why, we have to look beyond the averages.

During those periods in the past 30 years when S&P 500 returns have
been below average, 50 percent of actively managed large-cap U.S.
mutual funds actually beat the index. This phenomenon was not unique
to large-cap U.S. stocks. The relative performance of active managers
improved in every asset class when the returns were below average.
History shows that the stronger the performance of an asset class, the
more difficult it proves to be for active managers to outperform the index.

How does that affect the implementation of the portfolio strategy outlined in Part 2? If the returns for the U.S. stock and bond market over the
remainder of the decade are below the long-term average return (as I
forecast in Part I), then active large-cap U.S. stock managers may fare bet-

ter than they have, on average, over the past 30 years. In that scenario, incorporating some degree of active management may be of value.

As interest rates have fallen during the past 20 years, total returns have been above average for bonds. As a result, active managers have performed poorly versus the index, on average. However, during weaker periods of performance, active managers fared better. When interest rates were steadily rising in the 1970s, few bond mutual funds existed. From the inception of the Lehman Brothers U.S. Aggregate Bond Index in 1976 until the peak in interest rates in September of 1981, an average of 61 percent of the actively managed core U.S. bond mutual funds outperformed the Lehman Index on a rolling 12-month basis. The average actively managed municipal bond fund also outperformed the Lehman Municipal Bond Index over that period of rising interest rates.

What would the data show if we analyze the performance using different measurement periods? Using monthly data, rather than 12-month rolling periods, does not significantly change the percentage of active managers outperforming the index for most asset classes, but it does for U.S. bonds. For the past 20 years, bond yields have been falling and bond returns have been above average. The more granular monthly data reveals that, although interest rates generally declined over the entire period, interest rates rose 46 percent of the time on a monthly basis. Using monthly data, an average of 41 percent of active bond managers outperformed the Lehman Brothers Aggregate U.S. Bond Index during the past 20 years, compared to just 29 percent using rolling 12-month periods. Nearly 50 percent of active bond fund managers outperformed when monthly returns were below average. With rates near 40-year lows and the bond bull market at an end, I would expect active U.S. bond managers to fare better against their benchmarks over the next ten years than during the past 20 years. This argues for incorporating some active management of the bond asset classes.

As other asset classes become more efficient, a blended strategy of active and passive management that is similar to bonds and large-cap U.S. stocks may be appropriate. In the new era of investment performance, an active approach may be more rewarding than during the passive, buy-and-hold period of the 1990s. A mix of both active and passive investment vehicles may be the best way to implement the asset allocation in the years ahead.

The Quality of Earnings

Earnings are an opinion, but they are not a fantasy. The interpretation and application of accounting conventions result in a lot of flexibility financial officers can use to present corporate results. Different people can come to different conclusions as to exactly how much a company earned in a given year based on the same underlying results and accounting rules. Which measure is best depends upon the purpose for which it is calculated. For our purposes, focusing on operating earnings makes the most sense.

Operating versus Reported Earnings

Reported profits include the impact of recurring sales and costs but also incorporate the effects of non-recurring items. Nonrecurring items include the following:

- Merger and acquisition-related restructuring costs or write-offs. These are gains or losses from the sale of a division or the write-down of the value of an acquisition. When a company issues stock to acquire another company the price paid above the value of the assets of the acquired firm is called goodwill and recorded as an asset on the combined firm's balance sheet. The company may later take a non-cash charge and write-off of some, or all, of that goodwill if it finds that the value of the acquisition is now below the value carried on the balance sheet.

- Losses associated with discontinued operations. The costs of disposal of a division or the phase out of the operations.
- Extraordinary items, which are defined as events which are unusual and infrequent. These can include gains or losses on marketable securities held by the firm or the gain associated with refinancing debt at a lower interest rate, which creates an accounting gain.
- Gains or losses associated with accounting changes, made voluntarily (such as a change in the method of inventory valuation) or those mandated by new accounting standards.
- Operating earnings exclude these non-recurring, one-time write-offs. In the 1970s, there was no distinction between reported and operating earnings. In the mid-1980s the decline in inflation led to business restructuring which caused big write-offs as companies incurred one time expenses to re-orient their businesses to lower inflation. Analysts began adding these charges back to results to get a better sense of what the on-going or operating results of the companies actually were. It is useful that firms categorize expenses into operating and nonrecurring expenses, since it is the earnings prior to nonrecurring items that should be used when assessing the future earnings potential of a company. See Figure A.1.

The year-over-year change in earnings is distorted by the one time write-offs included in reported earnings. For example, a huge drop in earnings in one-quarter related to a non-cash accounting adjustment to a merger that may have taken place years ago will be followed by a sharp snapback, yet the actual operating results of the company were unaffected. I am not suggesting that write-offs should be completely ignored. If a company has frequent non-recurring charges, investors will probably see those write-offs as likely to recur and add them back in as part of the on-going operations of the business. Operating earnings, which reflect the trend in the main business operations of the company, are the best measure for investors to use in valuing companies on the basis of earnings.

Operating Earnings Track Economics

Charges that operating earnings are "earnings without the bad stuff" or that they are too liberal and foster systemic accounting fraud are not

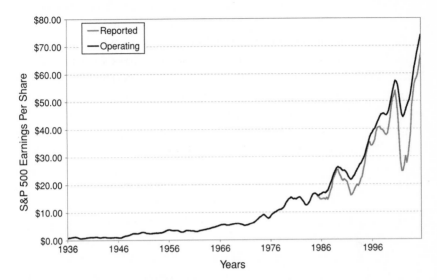

FIGURE A.1   Since the mid-1980s reported earnings have become more volatile than
operating earnings.
S&P 500 reported earnings per share and operating earnings per share .

supported by the data. S&P 500 operating earnings track economic data
such as industrial production and GDP. This suggests they measure the
actual economic output effectively. See Figure A.2.

Reported profits using GAAP do not tend to track economic fundamentals very well. This is because they do not exclude non-recurring
charges such as goodwill impairment (which have nothing to do with
the operating metrics such as sales and margins—instead they reflect
too much paid for M&A transactions in the 1990s rather than an over-
statement of prior earnings). Also, they introduce a lot of volatility into
the earnings numbers that do not reflect fundamentals. For example,
the write-offs in 2001 would have lowered earnings by about 50 percent in 2002. See Figure A.3.

In addition to GDP, the Bureau of Economic Analysis reports on
national income which includes a measure of corporate profits. Rather
than being based on financial accounting principles, the national
income measure of profits uses tax accounting principles. Both financial accounting and tax accounting methods calculate profits as the difference between revenues and expenses, but they differ with respect

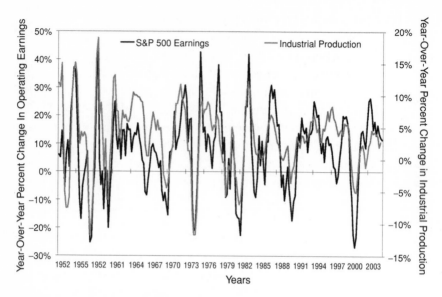

FIGURE A.2   Operating earnings have tracked industrial production.
S&P 500 operating earnings and industrial production.

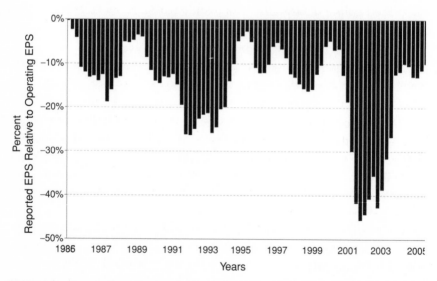

FIGURE A.3   Reported profits nearly 50% below operating as write-offs peaked in
                       2001 and 2002.
S&P 500 reported EPS relative to operating EPS on rolling four quarter basis.

to their definitions and the timing of when they are recorded. Annual tabulations from the IRS of corporate profits become available with a three year lag, when they are released the tax-based national income estimate is updated to reflect these tabulations. Because they are benchmarked to actual tax return information they can be considered a fairly conservative and accurate assessment of profits. Capital gains and losses are not included in the national income calculations measures because they result from the sale of existing assets rather than from current production and bad debt expenses are not deducted because these charges represent a rearrangement of assets and liabilities on a national basis rather than result from the costs of current production. Because they measure national income the data cover all US companies both pubic and private, while S&P 500 operating earnings only cover 500 large public companies in the United States. Nevertheless, when we adjust these tax-based NIPA profits for bad debt expense and capital gains they have correlated well with S&P 500 operating earnings over time.

Inflation and Earnings Quality

S&P 500 operating earnings provide a good input for earnings based approaches to valuation. However, no matter what measure is used, inflation has been the main enemy of earnings quality over time and it indiscriminately affects all the measures.

In the 1970s, companies' earnings were boosted by gains from the rising value of inventories as inflation soared. Also, the adjustment to earnings to account for the depreciation of plant and equipment under-represented the actual replacement cost of that capacity since the depreciation was based on historical cost (which was well below the inflated replacement cost). The understated deprecation resulted in the reporting of overstated and unsustainable accounting profits.

The current environment of low and stable inflation poses little risk to earnings quality, however, if inflation unexpectedly began to steadily climb a more conservative approach to measuring corporate earnings would be appropriate.

Index